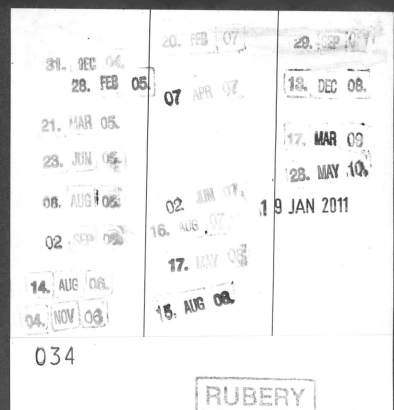

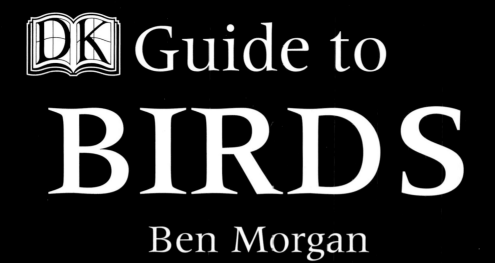

# DK Guide to
# BIRDS

## Ben Morgan

A Dorling Kindersley Book

LONDON, NEW YORK, MUNICH,
MELBOURNE, and DELHI

**Project Editor** Zahavit Shalev
**Art Editor** Jacqueline Gooden
**Editorial Assistant** Fleur Star
**Publishing Manager** Sue Leonard
**Managing Art Editor** Clare Shedden
**Category Publisher** Mary Ling
**DTP Designer** Almudena Díaz
**DTP Assistant** Pilar Morales
**Picture Research** Sarah Stewart-Richardson
**Jacket Design** Katy Wall
**Production** Shivani Pandey

**Consultant** Dr. Mark Fox,
Wild Animal Health MSc Course Co-Director,
The Royal Veterinary College

First published in Great Britain in 2004 by
Dorling Kindersley Limited
80 Strand, London WC2R 0RL

Penguin Group

2 4 6 8 10 9 7 5 3 1

Copyright © 2004 Dorling Kindersley Limited

A CIP catalogue record for this book
is available from the British Library

ISBN 1-4053-0248-8

Colour reproduction by GR3 Editrice, S.r.l., Verona

Printed and bound by
Mondadori Printing S.p.A., Verona, Italy

See our complete
catalogue at
**www.dk.com**

# CONTENTS

# WHAT IS A BIRD?

Birds are the most successful flying animals that have ever existed. They make up the scientific class *Aves*, distinguished from other animals by one feature: feathers. Birds almost certainly evolved from small, predatory dinosaurs called theropods more than 150 million years ago. Over time, the theropods' scales were transformed into feathers, their front legs stretched and became wings, their bony tails withered away, and their snouts and teeth were replaced by lightweight bills. Evolution made them masters of the sky, and they soon spread across the planet.

## A COAT OF FEATHERS

Birds are the only animals with feathers. These are not just for flight – they also provide a warm coat to trap heat in the body. Birds are warm blooded, which means they maintain a constant internal temperature, rather than warming up and cooling down with the surroundings, as happens in reptiles.

## FIRST BIRDS

The oldest bird fossil is that of *Archaeopteryx*, which lived about 150 million years ago and was a curious mixture of dinosaur and bird. *Archaeopteryx* had feathers like a modern bird, but teeth, a bony tail, and front claws like those of a *Velociraptor*.

## FITTING THE BILL

Bills (or beaks) evolved because they are lighter than toothed jaws and so make flying easier. They are also simpler than jaws, consisting merely of thin bone coated with the tough protein that forms human fingernails. As a result, evolution can change their shape relatively easily, giving each species a design adapted to its way of life. Flesh-eaters, for example, have hooked bills for tearing flesh.

IBIS

VULTURE

PARROT

TOUCAN

*Primary flight feathers produce the power for flying and are used for steering.*

*Secondary flight feathers provide lift.*

*Tertiary feathers shape the wing.*

## DIGESTIVE SYSTEM

Since they have no teeth, birds must break up food inside their bodies. They have a special stomach chamber called a gizzard, with powerful muscular walls that squeeze and grind the food. Less frequent flyers swallow grit or stones to help the gizzard do its job. Many birds also have a food storage chamber, or crop, in the throat. This helps them to wolf down food quickly and then bring it up again later to feed their chicks or to lose weight when fleeing danger.

PROVENTRICULUS

OESOPHAGUS

LARGE INTESTINE

CLOACA

SMALL INTESTINE

GIZZARD

CROP

*Boneless tail.*

*Warm blooded: body temperature 41-44°C (106-111°F).*

## SENSES

Vision is the most important sense in birds. Many can see colours invisible to our eyes or tiny details that we would need a telescope to notice. When they sleep, birds can keep one eye open and half the brain stays awake, wary for danger. Most birds have a poor sense of smell but excellent hearing. What sounds to us like a single note of birdsong might be heard by a bird as 10 separate notes.

*Powerful breast muscles to operate the wings.*

*No projecting ears or nose.*

*Large eyes and sharp vision.*

*Lightweight bill without teeth.*

*Compact, streamlined shape.*

*Downy feathers cover skin.*

*Thin legs with scaly skin.*

*Most birds have three forward-facing toes and one backward-facing toe.*

## GLOBAL DOMINATION

Flight has allowed birds to colonize almost every environment, from deserts and cities to remote islands, mountain peaks, and the freezing wastes of Antarctica. Birds can endure colder weather and thinner air than any other animals. The only habitat they haven't conquered is the deep sea.

RAINFOREST

WETLANDS

DESERT

MOUNTAINS

ARCTIC

TOWNS AND CITIES

## SMALL PERCHERS

Passerines, or perching birds, account for some 5,700 of the world's 9,700 bird species. Most of the birds that we see around our homes and gardens belong to this group.

*Passerines such as this blue tit have thin, grasping toes for perching on twigs.*

## REPRODUCTION

While mammals carry babies inside the body, birds lay eggs, like their reptilian ancestors. But, unlike most reptiles, which simply abandon their eggs, birds care for both eggs and chicks. Usually both parents cooperate to keep the young warm, and to protect and feed them.

# BUILT FOR FLIGHT

ALMOST EVERY PART OF A BIRD'S BODY has been shaped by evolution to meet
the demands of flight. Wings and feathers are the most obvious features –
they provide the "lift" to overcome gravity. Most birds also have a streamlined
shape with weight concentrated in the middle for balance. The bones are
riddled with hollow spaces to save on weight, and many are rigidly fused
together to reduce the need for heavy joints or unnecessary muscles. The
flight muscles are huge and powerful, but they need plenty of oxygen, so
birds have special lungs to extract as much oxygen as possible from the air.

*Outer vane
(windward edge
of feather)*

*Notch for reducing
turbulence*

### FEATHER LIGHT
Feathers are made of fine, lightweight
fibres of keratin, the protein that coats
bills. Flight feathers have a stiff central
shaft, called a quill, with hundreds of
side branches called barbs. The barbs
bear thousands of tiny branches
called barbules, which lock
together to form a flat,
streamlined surface.

*Inner vane
(leeward edge
of feather)*

*This magnified view
shows the feather's
central shaft, with
barbs branching off
the shaft and barbules
branching off the barbs.*

*Quill*

### THE BARE BONES
A bird's skeleton has the same basic
plan as a human skeleton, but the details
are very different. Birds have only three
"fingers" (digits), and these are fused to form a
strut supporting the wing. The wing pivots at
the shoulder, and the elbow and wrist can bend
only horizontally to fold or extend the wing.
The tail bones are fused into a stump, and
sidebars on the ribs overlap to form a solid cage.
An enormous bone called the keel provides an
anchor for the powerful flight muscles.

### ON THE WING
A bird's most important feathers
are its flight feathers, found on
the wings and tail. Most of the
lift required for flight is generated by
the primary and secondary flight feathers
in the outer part of the wing. There
are usually 9–12 of these on each wing.
Other parts of the body are covered with
small "contour feathers", which give the
bird a streamlined surface, or fluffy down
feathers, which keep the bird warm.

*Primary flight
feathers*

*Secondary
flight feathers*

*Tertiary flight
feathers*

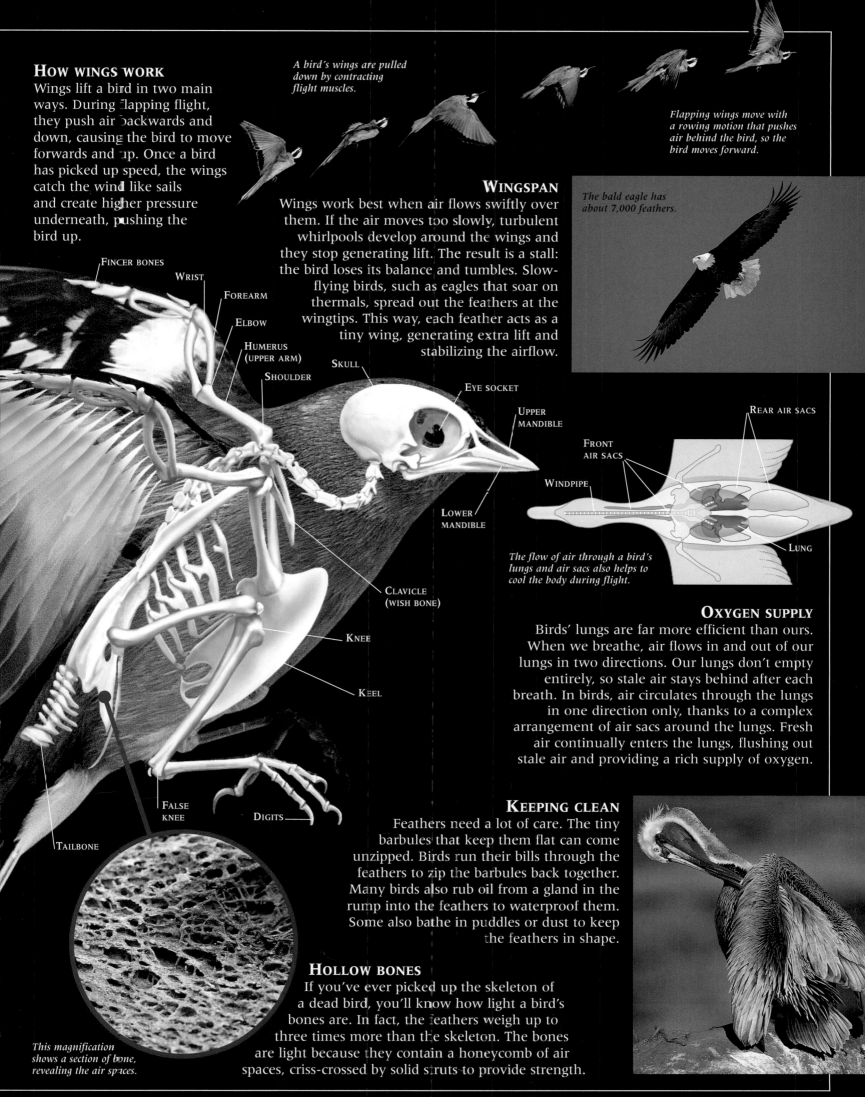

## HOW WINGS WORK

Wings lift a bird in two main ways. During flapping flight, they push air backwards and down, causing the bird to move forwards and up. Once a bird has picked up speed, the wings catch the wind like sails and create higher pressure underneath, pushing the bird up.

*A bird's wings are pulled down by contracting flight muscles.*

*Flapping wings move with a rowing motion that pushes air behind the bird, so the bird moves forward.*

## WINGSPAN

Wings work best when air flows swiftly over them. If the air moves too slowly, turbulent whirlpools develop around the wings and they stop generating lift. The result is a stall: the bird loses its balance and tumbles. Slow-flying birds, such as eagles that soar on thermals, spread out the feathers at the wingtips. This way, each feather acts as a tiny wing, generating extra lift and stabilizing the airflow.

*The bald eagle has about 7,000 feathers.*

FINGER BONES
WRIST
FOREARM
ELBOW
HUMERUS (UPPER ARM)
SHOULDER
SKULL
EYE SOCKET
UPPER MANDIBLE
WINDPIPE
LOWER MANDIBLE
CLAVICLE (WISH BONE)
KNEE
KEEL
FALSE KNEE
DIGITS
TAILBONE

FRONT AIR SACS
REAR AIR SACS
LUNG

*The flow of air through a bird's lungs and air sacs also helps to cool the body during flight.*

## OXYGEN SUPPLY

Birds' lungs are far more efficient than ours. When we breathe, air flows in and out of our lungs in two directions. Our lungs don't empty entirely, so stale air stays behind after each breath. In birds, air circulates through the lungs in one direction only, thanks to a complex arrangement of air sacs around the lungs. Fresh air continually enters the lungs, flushing out stale air and providing a rich supply of oxygen.

## KEEPING CLEAN

Feathers need a lot of care. The tiny barbules that keep them flat can come unzipped. Birds run their bills through the feathers to zip the barbules back together. Many birds also rub oil from a gland in the rump into the feathers to waterproof them. Some also bathe in puddles or dust to keep the feathers in shape.

## HOLLOW BONES

If you've ever picked up the skeleton of a dead bird, you'll know how light a bird's bones are. In fact, the feathers weigh up to three times more than the skeleton. The bones are light because they contain a honeycomb of air spaces, criss-crossed by solid struts to provide strength.

*This magnification shows a section of bone, revealing the air spaces.*

# UP AND AWAY

BIRDS MOVE THROUGH THE AIR with such grace that flying looks effortless to our eyes. But it takes tremendous effort to overcome the force of gravity and travel on nothing but air. For most birds, getting off the ground is the hardest part. Wings work best when air is blowing over them, so until a bird has built up speed it relies on muscle power alone. Once they get going, birds can conserve energy by catching the wind, gliding on air currents, or taking brief rests.

*A buzzard rides on a thermal, its wings outstretched to catch the rising air.*

## HITCHING A LIFT

Birds of prey and vultures soar to great heights by riding on upwellings of warm air called thermals. To stay in a thermal they have to keep turning, which is why they are often seen circling. After reaching the top of a thermal, they can glide for miles without having to flap.

*Puffins' short wings are better suited to swimming than flying, but they can take off with relative ease by jumping off cliffs.*

## JUMP START

Puffins get airborne by throwing themselves off cliffs. As they fall they pick up speed and their short wings begin to generate lift. They find it much harder taking off from the sea after diving for fish, however. To do so they must run across the water and beat their stubby wings as fast as they possibly can.

## FLIGHT PATTERNS

Birds differ a great deal in their style of flight. Small birds tend to flap intermittently and close their wings for barely perceptible rests. As a result, their flight paths move up and down. Ducks and geese are non-stop flappers. They are fast and have enormous stamina, but they use up energy quickly. Long-winged birds like vultures and albatrosses are gliders. They conserve energy by riding on thermals or catching the wind.

*Small birds such as finches have an up-and-down flight path because they shut their wings intermittently.*

FINCH FLIGHT PATTERN

*Ducks and geese flap their wings continuously and fly in a straight line.*

WATERFOWL FLIGHT PATTERN

*Birds of prey glide in circles on thermals to climb without wasting energy.*

WHITE TAILED EAGLE

## FLOCKING TOGETHER

Flying in a flock has several advantages. If each bird flies slightly to the side of the bird in front, it gets a lift from currents blowing off the leading bird's wings. This is why ducks and geese fly in V-formations. Flocks also make finding food easier and give protection from predators. Starlings sometimes flock by the thousand, forming dark clouds that twist and pulse as the birds swoop past each other in perfect co-ordination.

## LANDING

Landing takes less effort than taking off, but it requires skill – especially in birds that land on a small perch. To lose speed, birds bring their wings into a more vertical position and lower their tails. Many birds have a special tuft of feathers (the alula) on the bend of the wing that helps stabilize airflow over the wings as they slow down, keeping them balanced.

## GETTING AIRBORNE

It takes tremendous effort for a swan to get into the air. Its wings, like the wings of an aircraft, only generate sufficient lift when a fast stream of air is flowing past them. So to overcome gravity, the swan must sprint with all its strength, using the surface of the water as a runway. Facing the wind helps, but in still air a heavy swan has to reach about 48 kph (30 mph) to take off.

*The alula helps keep the bird stable as it slows down.*

*Water birds use their feet as brakes when they land.*

*The tail is lowered to act as a brake.*

# AERIAL ACROBATS

SWIFTS AND HUMMINGBIRDS SHARE A SPECIAL TYPE OF WING that makes them the most acrobatic of birds. Their "wrist" and "elbow" joints are very close to the body and their wings rotate at the shoulder. This gives superb flexibility and a very rapid wing beat. Swifts are among the fastest birds in level flight and can stay airborne for years. Hummingbirds can hover motionless and fly backwards or even upside down. To fuel their aerial stunts, these birds need a lot of food. Swifts trawl the air with their mouths agape to catch tiny midges; hummingbirds use their long bills to suck nectar from flowers.

## EUROPEAN SWIFT

The European swift is the world's most aerial animal and can stay airborne for two years at a time. It eats, drinks, sleeps, mates, and gathers nest material entirely on the wing. Its tiny legs are so feeble that it cannot walk, but it can cling to vertical surfaces.

*The swift's streamlined shape helps it catch insects in mid-air.*

## BEHIND THE WATERFALL

South America's great dusky swift builds its nest behind a waterfall and can fly straight through the raging torrent to reach it. Swifts can't land to gather nest material, so they build nests from a mixture of sticky spit and fluffy materials caught in the air. The nests of certain swifts are considered a delicacy in China and are boiled to make soup.

## A LIFE ON THE WING

Swallows and martins are not close relatives of swifts, but they are a similar shape and they also feed during flight. Their pointed wings and forked tails help them twist and turn with breathtaking agility as they chase flying insects one by one. They also drink on the wing, swooping low over ponds to take mouthfuls of water.

## TINY NESTS

Hummingbirds build tiny but deep cup-shaped nests from moss and spider's silk. The outside may be decorated with lichen for camouflage and the inside is lined with soft fibres. The bee hummingbird's nest is the size of a thimble.

### SMALLEST BIRD

The male bee hummingbird of Cuba is only 5.7 cm (2.2 in) long from bill to tail, making it the world's smallest bird. To stay airborne it must beat its wings an amazing 200 times a second, which produces a buzzing sound like a bee.

*Bee hummingbirds are so small and light that they often get trapped in spider's webs and die.*

*Hummingbirds' wings move so fast that they normally appear as a blur.*

*The long bill is used to reach nectar deep in the flower.*

### HOVERING HUMMER

Hummingbirds fly in a different way to other birds, twisting their wings back and forth in a figure-of-eight pattern rather than flapping them up and down. This motion allows a hummingbird to hover and stay perfectly still before pulling out of a flower. But the wings are short and must beat very quickly, which uses a great deal of energy.

*Hummingbirds have only about 1,000 feathers each – the fewest of any bird.*

*The sword-billed hummingbird's bill is nearly twice the length of its body.*

### FUELLED BY NECTAR

Hummingbirds use energy so quickly that they must visit up to 2,000 flowers a day. In doing so they unwittingly spread pollen between flowers and so help plants to reproduce. At night, hummingbirds go into a kind of hibernation to conserve energy.

# BIRDS OF PREY

FLESH IS THE MOST NUTRITIOUS type of food, but it is exceptionally hard to obtain. Nevertheless, the birds of prey, or raptors, have made killing and scavenging their way of life. There are around 300 species, and nearly all share the specialized features needed to hunt and butcher: superb vision, a vicious set of talons for killing their prey, and – as raptors cannot swallow prey whole as owls can – a hooked bill for stripping flesh.

### DADDY WITH DINNER
As with most birds of prey, the female red-tailed hawk guards the eggs and the young, and the father, who is smaller, does most of the hunting. The chicks spend about 48 days in the nest. In the last week they learn to use their wings by standing on the edge of the nest and flapping while facing the wind.

*Powerful, hooked bill for tearing flesh.*

### EAGLE EYE
A special pit in the back of each eye provides birds of prey with telephoto vision so sensitive they can spot the twitch of a rabbit's ears from up to 2 miles away. Our eyes focus on one point at a time, so we have to keep moving them to look around. Raptors have eyes that can focus on three zones at once: the horizon on each side and a single, magnified spot straight ahead.

*Huge eyes give goshawks razor-sharp vision. A ridge over the eye protects it and gives the bird a mean, glowering expression.*

*Huge, incurved talons for seizing prey. In many raptors, the rear talon is the strongest and deadliest*

## BALD EAGLE

Eagles are among the largest and most powerful raptors, built to overpower animals as big as sheep or even reindeer. Like owls, they often tear their victims' heads off before dismembering them. The bald eagle is truly a colossal bird with a wingspan greater than a man's height, but it feeds mainly on fish such as salmon.

## THE SPORT OF KINGS

In parts of central Asia, falconry with eagles is used as a way of getting food for people to eat, and not just for sport as in the West. The falconer trains the bird to take off from his arm, which is protected by a padded leather glove.

## FIVE FAMILIES

Experts can't agree how to classify the raptors, but most authorities split the 307 species into five families, shown below. Owls are not usually classed as birds of prey, but vultures are.

ANDEAN CONDOR

*American vultures and condors consist of seven species (Cathartidae) and include some of the largest flying birds.*

SECRETARY BIRD

*Africa's peculiar secretary bird is classified in a family of its own (Saggitaridae). It looks a bit like an eagle on stilts.*

BALD EAGLE

*Eagles, hawks, kites, harriers, and Old World vultures make up a family of over 200 species (Accipitridae).*

OSPREY

*The osprey is classed in a family of its own (Pandionidae) because it has an unusual reversible outer toe.*

FALCON

*About 60 species belong to this family (Falconidae). They have a kind of tooth on the upper bill and pointed wings.*

# BLOOD LUST

IT TAKES PRACTICE TO BECOME a proficient killer, so most birds of prey specialize in a particular strategy. For members of the eagle and hawk family, the principal weapons are the talons, which kill by puncturing the prey's body and inflicting mortal wounds. In contrast, falcons hold small prey in their talons and use the bill to snap the spine and cripple them. But whatever their technique, all birds of prey are opportunists and will steal or scavenge when necessary.

## SWOOP TO CONQUER

The peregrine falcon performs a stunning dive. It turns its body into a dart and plunges at up to 200 kph (124 mph), making it the fastest bird on Earth. As it closes in for the kill it leaves the dive, swings its feet forward, and shreds open the victim's back with an enlarged rear talon – the "killer claw".

*Peregrine falcons are successful on less than 1 in 10 of their dives.*

## BULLYING TACTICS

Bald eagles' fishing trips frequently end in failure, so sometimes a bird steals food from other raptors, including bald eagles. Giving chase is often enough to persuade another bird to drop its kill, but occasionally bald eagles will pick a fight, like these two juvenile birds.

*Juvenile bald eagles have brown feathers, which change to white head and black body feathers as they mature.*

### FISH FANCIER

Ospreys specialize in catching fish. They approach the water at a low angle, swing their feet forward, then plunge into the water to grasp the fish in their talons. For improved grip, they can swivel one of their toes round, giving them two forward-pointing and two backward-pointing toes. Their feet are covered with sharp scales that give them so much extra grip that they can become stuck to the fish and drown if the catch is too heavy.

*As it flies off, the osprey turns its catch to face forwards, which makes it easier to carry.*

### MONKEY EATER

Rainforest eagles have short wings so they can sneak through the forest canopy and take monkeys by surprise. The African crowned eagle smashes into its prey with heavy, clublike feet, delivering a blow ferocious enough to both impale and knock out its prey. This vervet monkey stood little chance against its attacker. If it wasn't killed instantly by the first blow, it would soon have succumbed to massive internal bleeding.

*An African crowned eagle can kill a monkey as heavy as itself.*

### DEATH BY STAMPING

Unusually for birds of prey, secretary birds are not very good at flying. They flush out prey by walking until they find something to kill and then they stamp it to death. They can kill snakes but they also eat insects, small animals like lizards or mice, or small eggs and birds.

*The secretary bird is one of the only birds of prey that can swallow prey whole.*

*Plucking is necessary as sparrowhawks cannot digest feathers.*

### PLUCKING POST

Stealth is essential to the sparrowhawk's technique. It flies along a hedgerow, hidden from its target on the other side. Then, with a deft wing flick, it darts over the hedge to pluck an unsuspecting songbird off its perch. Some hawks use a trick to subdue their prey: they push their powerful rear claw into the victim's skull and puncture the brain, causing instant death. The victim is often taken to a plucking post to be stripped of its feathers.

# SCAVENGERS

MANY BIRDS WILL HAPPILY TUCK into a corpse, but the best-known scavengers of the bird world are the vultures. Circling high on thermals, they scan the ground for signs of death. They are attracted to the sick, the injured, and the commotion caused by hunting. They also spy on each other – so when one finds a carcass, others soon follow from miles around.

## MARABOU STORK

The marabou stork of Africa is a wading bird that has turned to scavenging. As well as muscling in on flocks of vultures, it lingers near fires to catch animals fleeing the heat. Its legs are stained white by excrement, which it squirts on itself to keep cool. The fine white feathers lining its tail used to be much in demand to decorate hats.

## TOO FULL TO FLY

White-backed vultures are the most common vultures in Africa and often the first to locate a carcass. They cram so much food into their crops that they can barely fly. After eating, they flap awkwardly into a tree and rest while the meal is digested.

## FEEDING FRENZY

African vultures can strip an antelope to the bone in as little as 20 minutes. Small griffon or white-backed vultures are usually first on the scene and quickly cover the body in a scrum, squabbling noisily as they shove past each other. Larger marabou storks and lappet-faced vultures arrive later but take priority because they are stronger. Any bones left afterwards are crushed and eaten by hyenas.

## STRONG STOMACH

The lammergeier prefers bones to flesh. Strong acid in its stomach dissolves the hard, outer part of a bone and releases the rich marrow inside. If the bones are too big to swallow, the lammergeier drops them onto rocks to smash them open. It can drop the same bone several times if it does not break on the first attempt.

## SINISTER AND SILENT

The turkey vulture is unusual in finding food by smell rather than sight – a distinct advantage in the dense forests of the Amazon, where bodies are hidden from view. It is one of the few birds that has no syrinx (voicebox) and so cannot sing. Between meals, flocks roost together in dead trees in sinister silence.

*Like other birds of prey, most vultures have a hooked bill for tearing flesh.*

## RAVENOUS RAVENS

Ravens scavenge mainly in winter, when other animals succumb to the cold and lack of food. People have long seen ravens and their relatives – crows and magpies – as symbols of evil, but they are intelligent and inquisitive birds. Unlike vultures, ravens cooperate and seem to tell each other where to find food.

## EGG CRACKERS

The Egyptian vulture is not just a scavenger, but an egg thief. It knows how to crack even the thick-shelled eggs of ostriches by gripping a heavy stone in its beak and hurling it against the egg. Ravens and crows use a different technique, carrying eggs to a height and dropping them.

## BALD AND UGLY

Most vultures have bald heads and necks so that they can push their way deep inside a carcass without soiling their plumage. Baldness is also useful when living in a hot climate, as heat trapped by body feathers escapes through the bare skin.

# PARTNERS AND PARASITES

S OMETIMES IT PAYS FOR A BIRD to form a special partnership with another species. By teaming up, they might be able to find food that neither could reach alone or defend themselves against a predator. Different bird species sometimes cooperate to drive away birds of prey; for instance small birds might "mob" an owl. In Africa, honeyguide birds team up with people to find and raid bees' nests. When both partners benefit like this, the relationship is called symbiosis. Not all close partnerships work out so fairly, however. Often one partner takes advantage of the other: it becomes a parasite.

### EGG MIMICS
Birds that sneak their eggs in others' nests are called brood parasites. The most successful brood parasites lay eggs that mimic their host's eggs. If the eggs are a poor match, like these cuckoo eggs, the nest's owner may realize and throw them out.

*The honeyguide is the only known creature that can digest beeswax.*

### HONEYGUIDE
The greater honeyguide has a taste for beeswax. It leads African tribespeople to wild bees' nests by flying in short stages and making a special call. The people smoke out the nest with burning leaves, take the honey, and throw a chunk of wax to the honeyguide as a reward.

*This cuckoo chick is a giant compared to its foster parents. Although it has outgrown the nest, the chick continues to be fed by the tiny reed warblers.*

### GARDENER'S FRIEND?
The European robin is not really being friendly as it hops about the feet of gardeners – it has learnt to search freshly dug soil for grubs. In Africa close relatives of robins, called alethes, use a similar technique, loitering around columns of marauding army ants to snatch insects fleeing their path.

### CRAFTY CUCKOOS
The common cuckoo always lays its eggs in other birds' nests. The cuckoo chick is usually first to hatch. Although it is bigger than the other chicks, the parents think it is their own. The sight of its huge red mouth begging for food triggers their parental instincts, and they cannot help but feed it.

### ANT BATH
Jays have the curious habit of lying on anthills and letting the angry ants scurry all over them. They allow ants to squirt defensive secretions over their feathers, which is thought to help reduce the number of parasites.

## FRIEND OR FOE?

Oxpeckers live on big game
animals, such as zebras.
They pick parasitic ticks
and lice from the fur,
providing what appears
to be a useful service.
But the oxpeckers are
parasites themselves – they
feed on earwax and blood,
and they peck at wounds
to keep them bleeding.

*Oxpeckers groom their hosts
in the most intimate spots,
creeping deep into nostrils
and ears.*

## CLEANING STATION

In the Galapagos Islands,
Darwin's finches provide a cleaning
service for giant tortoises. The tortoise
stretches its neck in response to being
touched on the leg by the finch. Then
the birds fly into the shell to pick blood-
sucking parasites off its wrinkly skin.

# FISHER KINGS

T O CATCH A FISH YOU NEED patience, a sharp eye, and lightning reactions. But most of all you need the element of surprise. For some birds, this means standing motionless in water until a fish blunders into range. Others attack from the air, performing a spectacular plunge-dive and striking before the victim has time to react.

## FISH SCOOP

The brown pelican uses two tricks to catch fish. First, it plunge-dives into the water, dropping from a height of 10 m (30 ft) and hitting the surface with a terrific splash. Then it uses an enormous throat pouch to scoop up fish. The pouch also takes in lots of water, so the pelican must rest on the surface afterwards to let the water out before swallowing its catch.

## SKIMMING THE SURFACE

Skimmers fly very close to the surface of lakes, rivers, and lagoons keeping their specially enlarged lower bill wide open in the water. If anything touches the bill – a fish, for example – it snaps shut automatically.

*Fish get sucked into the pouch with a rush of seawater. The edges of the pouch then close and trap the fish inside.*

*The pouch holds three times as much as the pelican's stomach.*

## KINGFISHER

The European kingfisher sits by a river as patiently as a fisherman, watching for prey to swim into striking range. At the sight of a small fish, it springs off its perch, hovers for a few seconds, and plunges into the water to snatch the fish with split-second precision. A powerful beat of the wings lifts it clear of the water again, firmly gripping its prey. A kingfisher may need to catch up to 50 fish a day to feed its young.

*Darters' feathers become waterlogged in water, helping them sink below the surface.*

## SPRING-LOADED NECK

Indian darters impale fish on their pointed beaks. Their necks are normally folded back in a z-shape but can straighten out with explosive speed to drive the tip of the beak straight through a fish. The darter tosses off the fish with a flick of the head and swallows it whole. Darters are also known as "snakebirds" thanks to their habit of swimming with only a long snake-like neck visible above the water.

## FISHERMAN'S UMBRELLA

Herons also use spring-loaded necks to hunt, but they strike from above the water. The black heron spreads its wings into an umbrella to cast a shadow over the water. This habit is called "mantling". Fish are naturally drawn into the shade, and the lack of reflection probably helps the heron peer through the surface and see its prey.

## PATIENT FISHER

The extraordinary shoebill stork catches fish and frogs in muddy African swamps. It can stand still for hours on end waiting for something edible to come into view, at which point it gets very excited and hurls itself at the animal. The enormous bill chops up the prey like a giant pair of scissors.

## DIVE BOMBER

Gannets and boobies hit the water like missiles. They dive from amazing heights, accelerating as they plunge and folding their wings right back at the very last moment to form a streamlined torpedo. They strike the water at up to 95 kph (60 mph) and often shoot straight past the shoal they are targetting. When that happens, they simply turn around and swim back up, snapping at fish on the way.

*The bill's hooked tip is used to pull animals out of mud.*

# BESIDE THE SEA

Living by the sea has great advantages for a bird. Most of the Earth is covered in water, and it is full of rich pickings. It is also true that craggy coastlines and islands provide a safe haven from the predators – human and animal – that are common inland. Some seabirds always stay close to the shore, searching for worms, shellfish, and other invertebrates in the shallow water and sand. Others make epic voyages to hunt the open ocean for fish. Kept aloft by the strong sea breezes, they can spend months on the wing, only alighting on land for short periods to breed or feed their chicks.

*A frigate bird attempts to steal food from a brown booby.*

### PIRATES OF THE AIR
Frigate birds are the pirates of the world's tropical oceans. In the air they are as swift and agile as any bird of prey, yet their plumage is not waterproof and they cannot swim. So instead of diving for fish themselves, they attack other birds returning from fishing trips and force them to regurgitate and give up their catch.

### ALBATROSS
At 3.5 m (11.5 ft) across – twice the height of a man – the wandering albatross has the greatest wingspan of any bird. Wings spread out to catch the wind, it glides effortlessly for miles, even sleeping on the wing. It can fly around the world on a single fishing trip.

### SEABIRD CITIES
Many seabirds nest in noisy, smelly colonies, like this horde of Cape gannets in South Africa. Thousands of birds come here every year to breed and raise a single chick. When the breeding season ends, the gannets disperse and the colony disappears.

## GULL GATHERING

Seagulls have an uncanny knack of finding fish in miles of apparently empty water. Their secret lies in being nosy: when one spots a shoal of fish and begins feeding, nosy neighbours are sure to follow. Many seagulls scavenge for food as well as hunting. In some seaside towns in England, the local gulls have learnt to dive-bomb people and snatch food from their hands.

*A shoal of fish driven to the surface by underwater predators attracts a frenzy of activity as seagulls arrive from miles around to pick them off.*

BLACK OYSTERCATCHER

SANDERLING

AMERICAN AVOCET

TURNSTONE

## LIFE'S A BEACH

Shorebirds generally have stilt-like legs for wading and long beaks for probing, but each species feeds in its own way. Oystercatchers pull up mussels and smash or split them by pecking. Sanderlings scamper back and forth over breaking waves, picking out tiny animals that get stranded. Avocets swing their curved beaks in muddy water and feel for shrimps, and turnstones flip pebbles over to find small crabs.

## ATLANTIC PUFFIN

With their sad eyes and seemingly painted faces, Atlantic puffins look rather like clowns. Their stubby wings beat with a whirring, propellor motion that seems clumsy in the air, but they double as highly effective flippers underwater, enabling these amphibious birds to dive to depths of up to 60 m (200 ft). The large bill is particularly colourful during the mating season. It has spiny edges and can hold as many as 60 fish at once.

# WADERS AND FLOATERS

VISIT A WETLAND OR A LAKE and you're sure to see lots of birds poking around in the shallows or swimming on the surface. Unlike mammals, birds have been very successful in adapting to freshwater habitats. While beavers and otters have to submerge completely to travel and hunt in water, birds keep themselves warm and dry by wading on stilt-like legs, floating on the surface, or probing the water only with their long beaks or necks. And when food gets hard to find, water birds can simply fly away and make a new home elsewhere.

*Flamingos get their colour from pigments in their food.*

## FLAMINGO FIESTA

Millions of flamingos congregate on the salt lakes of east Africa, forming vast pink slicks that are visible from the sky. In the breeding season their courtship dances are a breathtaking spectacle as thousands of birds nod and bow in unison.

*A flamingo's false knee bends backwards.*

## FILTER FEEDERS

Flamingos use their unusual bills to collect microscopic organisms from water. They place their heads upside down in the lake and use the tongue to pump water across a sieve inside the bill. Shrimp, algae, and bacteria are filtered out of the water and swallowed. This way of feeding allows flamingos to live in salty lakes where no other animals can survive.

## LONG LEGS

The stilt is the bird with the longest legs in relation to its body size. It can search for food in much deeper water than other small waders, but in shallow water it has to bend awkwardly to reach the mud. Its legs are too long to be tucked away in flight, so the stilt flies with them trailing elegantly behind it.

## FEEDING BY TOUCH

In murky water, the best way to find food is not by sight, but by touch. Spoonbills sweep their broad bills from side to side and snap them shut if anything enters. Sometimes they advance in a line and herd fish into a corner. Ibises poke their longer bills into mud and feel for worms and crabs.

## FOOD COLOURING

Scarlet ibises and pink flamingos get their colour from chemicals called carotenoids, which are also found in carrots. Carotenoids are made by algae in the water. The algae are either swallowed directly by the birds, or passed on inside via shrimps and worms that eat them.

## WATERPROOF COAT

Birds that float rather than wade, such as swans, ducks and geese, have boat-shaped bodies and webbed feet for swimming. To protect their feathers from water they smear them with waterproof oil from a gland on the rump. This "preen oil" makes water slide off in shiny pearls.

*Many ducks hunt by dabbling (upending) – heads go into the water, and tails up in the air.*

## SMOOTH OPERATOR

Though clumsy on land, some water birds become as nimble as otters when they disappear underwater. The goosander can catch salmon and trout – which is why fishermen hate it. Loons also dive for fish and can spend minutes underwater and reach 30 m (100 ft) deep. They are so well adapted to life on water that they cannot walk on land.

# BIRD FOOD

RICH, EASILY DIGESTED FOOD MAKES UP THE BULK of most birds' food. Because they need lots of energy, but have to keep their weight down for flight, very few birds eat bulky plant food such as grass or leaves. The majority are omnivores, taking a mix of seeds, fruit, and small animals including insects. Without teeth to grind and chew, birds must make do with their bills and their muscular stomachs. And they must digest their meals as quickly as possible to get rid of any excess weight.

*A blue tit enjoys a snack provided by a thoughtful bird-lover.*

## INSATIABLE APPETITE

Small birds burn energy at an amazing rate and must eat vast amounts just to stay warm, let alone fly. In winter, a blue tit can spend 90 per cent of its waking hours feeding to stay alive. Hummingbirds use up fuel at 10 times the rate humans do.

*A herring gull drops a mussel onto a rocky beach.*

## DROPPED FROM A HEIGHT

Foods encased in a shell can be problematic when a bird's bill lacks the power to crack them. One solution is to drop them from a height. This tactic is used by herring gulls on mussels, by lammergeiers to break bones, and by crows to smash eggs.

*A collared dove chick takes crop milk from its mother's throat.*

*Jays bury acorns in autumn to provide a supply of food in winter.*

*A jay can't swallow a whole acorn. Instead it wedges the acorn in a hole and pecks at it to split the shell.*

## FEAT OF MEMORY

Food is hard to find in winter, so some birds build up a secret stash during the autumn glut. Jays bury thousands of acorns, hiding each one in a different part of the forest and memorizing its location. Nutcrackers bury up to 100,000 nuts and seeds each year and can remember their locations nine months later.

## PIGEON MILK

Pigeons and doves are unique among birds in that they produce a kind of milk from the crop to feed their young. Crop milk, a thick soup of protein and fat, is made for the first three weeks of the chicks' lives. After that the mother weans them onto solid food by swallowing mouthfuls of seeds and storing them in the crop, where they soak in the milk to form porridge.

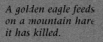
*A golden eagle feeds on a mountain hare it has killed.*

## BIG EATER

The golden eagle tackles the largest prey of any bird. In Scandinavia, it is said to kill reindeer up to 35 kg (77 lbs) in weight – about the size of a 10-year-old child. It kills by grasping the head with one set of talons and puncturing vital organs with the other.

## SPIKED BY A SHRIKE

Birds can't store as much body fat as mammals can because they need to keep their weight down for flight. A better way to store excess food is to hoard it, and this is what shrikes do. They keep a grisly larder of dead bodies impaled on thorns or barbed wire. Most shrikes collect insects, but this red-backed shrike has captured a lizard, and the great grey shrike also has mice and even birds in its larder.

## QUICK DIGESTION

An average meal takes half an hour to pass through a bird's body (compared to 24 hours in humans). A turkey vulture, for instance, can digest a whole snake in 90 minutes; the reverse process (a snake digesting a turkey vulture) takes weeks.

*Droppings are a mixture of white uric acid (concentrated urine) and black faeces.*

## EAT DIRT

Small birds hull their seeds to avoid carrying extra weight, but bigger seed-eaters such as farmyard chickens swallow seeds, husks and all. They grind up their meals in the gizzard, a muscular stomach that contains swallowed grit and stones to mash the food. A wood duck's gizzard can puree walnuts, and an eiderduck's can crush mussel shells. Turkeys are said to be able to grind steel needles in theirs.

# PARROT FAMILY

NOT MANY ANIMALS CAN SWEAR or tell a person to shut up, but parrots can – though whether they understand what they say is another matter. There are over 300 species in the parrot family, including macaws, lorikeets, budgies, and cockatoos. Most live in the lush forests of the tropics, where sound is a vital way of staying in touch with the flock. Parrots are instinctively friendly and bond with their companions by mimicking them. Wild parrots never mimic other species, so perhaps tame parrots see humans as members of their flock.

### PARROT PETS
Budgerigars have been kept as pets for over 100 years. Today they are bred in a multitude of colours and can be trained to talk and sit on their owners' fingers. Wild budgies are green and yellow. They live in inland Australia where they sometimes form flocks so vast they are said to darken the sky.

### PARROT FEATURES
The most distinctive feature of parrots is the hooked bill, which is used for scooping up fruit and cracking open nuts or seeds. Parrots have a powerful bite and use their beaks as grappling hooks while climbing. Their feet are also unusual, with two toes that point forwards and two that point backwards. This arrangement allows them to use one foot like a hand while perching safely on the other.

*A macaw's bill is strong enough to snip a person's finger off.*

*Parrots are the only birds that can lift food to their mouths with a foot.*

### MACAWS
The biggest parrots are the macaws, from the rainforests of Central and South America. Many species are named for their brilliant colours. The scarlet macaw, for instance, is a shocking red with flashes of blue and yellow. Their beautiful plumage and powers of mimicry have made macaws popular as pets, but in captivity they can become lonely and bored, leading to aggressive behaviour.

### FLIGHTLESS ODDITY
The kakapo of New Zealand lost its ability to fly because it had no need to flee from predators: there were no mammals in New Zealand for millions of years. It was even safe for the bird to live in a burrow. Now it is almost extinct, a victim of the animal predators brought by human settlers to the island.

*Kakapos come out of their burrows at night and waddle about looking for fresh grass to eat.*

## CURE FOR INDIGESTION

Nearly all parrots eat plant matter – usually seeds, nuts, fruit, or nectar. In the Amazon rainforest, many of the seeds that macaws eat are laced with poison, yet macaws have found an ingenious way of digesting these seeds without coming to harm. After a meal, they visit riverbanks to gnaw and swallow clay. The clay contains a mineral that absorbs the poisonous chemicals.

## RAINBOW LORIKEET

This dazzling little bird is one of the most colourful animals on Earth. It lives in the forests of Australia and the Pacific, where it feeds on the fruits, seeds, and the nectar of tropical flowers. Its tongue ends in a brush for soaking up nectar.

## ANGRY COCKATOO

Cockatoos and cockatiels are parrots with crests. They express anger or excitement by raising their crests. Cockatoos are popular as pets, but some have a tendency to bond with only one person and act aggressively to everyone else.

# BIRDS IN THE WOODS

Woodland birds can find everything they need in trees: safety from predators, shelter from the weather, holes to nest in, and an endless supply of food – provided they know where to look. Unsurprisingly, many birds have made forests their permanent home. The most specialized tree-dwellers are the woodpeckers, whose feet can grip vertical trunks and whose amazing, chisel-like bills can drill into wood to hollow out nests, chase wood-boring grubs, and send rattling calls echoing through the trees.

### TREE CREEPERS

European tree creepers hop their way up tree trunks using their bills as tweezers to pull insects out of crevices. To perch on vertical surfaces they cling tightly to the bark using their stiff tail as a prop just like woodpeckers do. Tree creepers can even walk upside down on the bottom of branches.

*The sheath wraps tightly around the skull to push the tongue out.*

*The sheath moves away from the skull to pull the tongue in.*

### TONGUE ACTION

Woodpeckers pull insects out of holes with a sticky tongue that extends to up to four times the length of the bill. The tongue's base connects to a flexible sheath that circles the skull. In some species this curls right round to an anchor point under the nostrils. A muscle pulls the sheath tight against the skull to push the tongue out.

### TREE VAMPIRES

The sapsucker is a kind of tree vampire. It drills shallow pits in the bark of trees and uses a feathery tongue to soak up the sap that oozes out. If the pits fully encircle the trunk, they can eventually cut off the tree's food supply and kill it.

### AT HOME IN A HOLE

Holes drilled in trees make the perfect place to raise chicks – they are warm, dry, and safe from any predator too big to crawl inside. Green woodpeckers use the same hole for up to 10 years.

### HAMMER HEAD

A woodpecker's beak can strike wood at 40 kph (25 mph). Such a blow would knock another bird unconscious but woodpeckers can hammer away 20 times a second and 10,000 times a day. Their brains are protected by a very thick skull and shock-absorbing muscles, and the rigid bill locks shut to stop it crumpling.

## ACORN LARDER

Acorn woodpeckers accurately drill different sized holes in a tree and hammer an acorn firmly into each one. Together, a family – consisting of up to 15 members of different generations – can build up a larder of 50,000 acorns in a single tree, providing enough food to see them through winter. The larder needs constant upkeep because the acorns slowly dry out, shrink, and have to be moved to smaller holes to stop them falling out.

*A male yellow-billed hornbill brings a meal to his imprisoned family.*

## TOCO TOUCAN

Toucans are close relatives of woodpeckers, but live only in the tropics. Their outsized bills look heavy, but are actually hollow and light. The toco toucan uses its bill to reach for fruits on the tips of twigs or to pull chicks out of nest holes. To get food into its throat, it tosses its head back and catches the food with its tongue.

## IMPRISONED IN A TREE

Female hornbills seal themselves inside their nest holes by blocking the entrance with mud, leaving only a narrow slit for the male to pass in food. The female spends about three months imprisoned in her home before breaking out to help gather food for the chicks.

# FEATHERS AND FINERY

Feathers are not just for flying – they are also for attracting attention. In the breeding season birds, unlike drably coloured mammals, flaunt brilliant colours, oversized tails, and all manner of decorations to impress the opposite sex. The showiest birds of all are males that mate with lots of partners. They contribute little to raising families, and devote all their energy to showing off. Their glossy colours and elaborate displays perform a vital function, advertising the excellence of their genes.

*A quetzal is about the size of a large pigeon, not including its tail.*

*The wild birds have black heads and purple breasts, but captive Gouldians are more colourful.*

## COAT OF MANY COLOURS
The vivid colours of the Gouldian finch have made this Australian bird irresistible to trappers and breeders. Only a few thousand remain in the wild today.

## A LENGTHY TAIL
Central America's resplendent quetzal has tail streamers more than a metre (3 ft) long and a coat of brilliant, metallic green. The Aztecs worshipped quetzals and made it a capital offence to kill them. Today the quetzal is the national bird of Guatemala.

*At the tip of each tail feather is a black eyespot ringed with blue and bronze. Eyespots attract attention because animals find them startling.*

## A PUZZLING TAIL
Scientists don't know why the peacock's large and cumbersome tail evolved. It is a serious handicap, hampering flight and making males conspicuous to predators, yet females love it! One explanation is that glossy plumage is a sign of health and therefore of good genes. Another theory is that females choose large-tailed males so their sons will be equally well-endowed.

PEACOCK    ROYAL FLYCATCHER    AMERICAN KING VULTURE

## ACE FACES
Sensational wings and tails are not always enough to impress a mate. Peacocks complement their tails with a blue head-crest, while royal flycatchers have a crest that retracts when they need to hide. American king vultures have featherless heads but startling eye rings, luridly coloured skin, and a fleshy orange flap over the bill.

### SEDUCTIVE SONG

The superb lyrebird of Australia displays his gauzy tail by draping it over his head to form a canopy. Then he begins a complex song in which he mimics everything from kookaburras and car alarms to mobile phones and chainsaws.

### IRIDESCENT PLUMAGE

Like many birds, ocellated turkeys have feathers that glint and change colour as they move. The feathers are "iridescent" – they reflect and split white light into different colours like soap bubbles and CDs do.

*Male Cabot's tragopan in full, startling display.*

### WHAT A WATTLE!

This colourful wattle – a flap of skin on the neck – is normally folded away. The male Cabot's tragopan exposes it with his head vibrating and his two blue horns erect to impress a nearby female.

### PRETTY PLUMES

Great egrets of both sexes grow ornamental plumes to impress each other in the breeding season. In the 19th century, hats sporting egret feathers were the height of fashion, and egrets were hunted almost to extinction. The hats have since gone out of fashion, and egrets have returned to the southern USA.

# THE MATING GAME

BIRDS, LIKE ALL ANIMALS, are driven by the urge to reproduce. Choosing the right partner is of vital importance, so birds have evolved rituals and displays that help them assess the opposite sex. Usually the female gets to choose and the male strives to impress her. She has to choose a partner of the same species, and this is why most birds, especially males, have distinctive calls and markings. Next, the male must prove he is a good catch using every trick in the book, from bringing gifts to singing love songs, dancing, or battling with his rivals.

### DANCING COUPLES

When courting herons meet, they perform a dance-like ritual, bending and straightening their necks and clashing their beaks together. Such behaviour looks odd to us, but it is full of signals that only the herons can understand. It helps them overcome their wariness of strangers, and strengthens the bond between them. Like most birds, herons are monogamous, which means that couples stay together to raise a family.

### BUILDING A BOWER

As a substitute for showy feathers, bowerbirds collect colourful objects and arrange them around a stack of twigs. Satin bowerbirds are particularly choosy, collecting only blue objects. Females mate with the males who produce the most artistic displays.

### FIGHTING FIT

Male birds don't win mates simply by looking beautiful – they have to prove their superiority over rivals, even if it means a fight to the death. Male golden pheasants slash at each other with the vicious spurs on the feet, but they usually settle their disputes without serious injury.

### LOOK AT ME!

Frigate birds attract attention from females by inflating a scarlet neck pouch until it is as big as a person's head and looks sure to burst. On some tropical islands the males congregate on trees, clustered like enormous ripe fruits. When females fly past, the males clack their bills, wave their wings about wildly, and make a strange gobbling noise.

## COURTSHIP CLOTHES

The male Count Raggi's bird of paradise has a fountain of gauzy red tail feathers that he fluffs and shakes while rolling around a branch and hanging upside down. But who is he trying to impress? Although females take a great interest in the display, it may actually be directed at other males. Groups of males gather and display together in the same tree, and in this way, seem to establish a ranking system. Visiting females always head straight to the top male.

*Gifts of food are a key part of the common tern's courtship. If the courtship is successful, the birds will probably stay together for life.*

## GIFT GIVING

Some male birds give presents to prospective mates. Male herons bring nest material, offered with much ceremonial bowing, and snowy owls offer freshly killed lemmings. Gifts of food are of more than symbolic value. They allow the female to assess how well her partner will feed future offspring, and they provide her with the valuable nutrients she needs to produce eggs.

*Blue-cheeked bee eaters, like many other birds, mate in a matter of seconds.*

## A BRIEF AFFAIR

Courtship is often a long and complex affair, but mating itself is usually very brief. The male flutters onto the female's back and the two birds press their genital openings together, allowing sperm to pass from male to female.

# MASTER BUILDERS

W ITH ONLY INSTINCT TO GUIDE THEM and only bills to serve as tools, birds construct nests of amazing complexity. A nest may take weeks to build and involve thousands of flights in search of suitable material. Some birds use whatever comes to hand – even string, nails, plastic bags, or old clothes. Others are much fussier. Hummingbirds build nests from spider's silk one strand at a time, while swallows collect a certain kind of mud from the edge of puddles.

*Lichen is used for camouflage.*

### CUP NEST
Most birds use a sequence of movements to create a cup-shaped nest with a snug hollow in the middle. First, they roughly organize the material, with softer items like feathers on the inside. Then they sit in the nest, and turning round and round, push themselves against it to form a perfectly sized cup.

*Straw and stiff fibres hold the nest together.*

*Feathers provide warmth.*

### COMMUNAL LIVING
In the deserts of southern Africa, sociable weaver birds build gigantic straw nests that house up to 100 families. From a distance they look like haystacks dropped on trees, but close inspection reveals a gallery of entrance tunnels on the underside. The nests can last for 100 years, and they provide both a cool refuge from midday heat and a warm shelter on chilly nights.

*Telegraph poles provide an alternative to trees in barren parts of the desert.*

### WOVEN HOME
Usually females do most of the nest-building, but in weaver birds the males do the work and females choose mates by inspecting their craftsmanship. Weavers are superb nest-builders and can tie knots by using their beaks and feet together. Like all birds, they work entirely from instinct, which means they know exactly how to construct a nest without ever being shown.

### TREE HOUSES

Woodpeckers make their homes by drilling holes in trees with their chisel-like bills. Boring through solid wood is hard work, so males and females work together, taking up to a month to complete the task. Instead of lining the nest with soft feathers or leaves, they finely chip the inner wall to make a cushion of sawdust.

*A male great spotted woodpecker delivers food to his family.*

*Birds that nest in colonies keep a careful distance from their neighbours.*

### LESS IS MORE

For many seabirds, a nest is little more than a scrape in the ground or a rocky ledge on a cliff. Gentoo penguins build simple mounds of pebbles, sticks, and grass. To impress their mates, the males collect pebbles of the same size and colour and arrange them in a neat ring around the nest.

*A tightly woven hem around the entrance stops this nest from unravelling.*

*The grosbeak weaver uses tough fibres torn from a particular type of grass. It weaves them into a wickerwork ball, slung between two plant stems.*

 MALLEE FOWL

 BARN SWALLOW

BEE EATER

### OUT OF HARM'S WAY

Many birds go to great lengths to keep their nests out of predators' reach. Mallee fowl bury their eggs under an enormous mound of rotting leaves, which not only hides the eggs, but keeps them warm. Barn swallows nest high under the eaves of buildings in a cup of mud and straw lined with grass and feathers. Carmine bee eaters burrow their way into sandy river banks and live in large colonies, where many eyes and ears can remain on the alert for danger.

*Mud nests are built one mouthful at a time and left to dry in the sun.*

### MUD HUT

Providing it stays dry, mud is an excellent nesting material. Ovenbirds use a mixture of mud, dung, and straw that sets rock hard under the sun, keeping out all but the strongest egg thieves. Their dome-shaped huts always face away from the wind and have an ingenious barrier inside the entrance to block draughts.

# EGGS

**A**LL BIRDS LAY EGGS rather than giving birth to live young as mammals do. This is because birds need to keep their weight down in order to fly, so mothers must get rid of their offspring as soon as they can. An egg, therefore, serves as an external womb, containing all the nutrients that a chick will need to develop. Parents simply keep their eggs warm, protect them from predators, and wait for them to hatch. We think of eggs as fragile, but in fact they are surprisingly tough: ostrich eggs are strong enough to stand on.

HUMMINGBIRD EGG

*Tiny as it looks, this egg is pretty hefty in proportion to the adult bird.*

## EXTRAORDINARY EGGS

Eggs are surprisingly varied and many are very different from the chicken eggs we eat. They range in size from hummingbird eggs the size of your little fingernail, to ostrich eggs, which are bigger than pineapples. Shapes range from cones to spheres (spherical eggs are strongest), and textures vary from rough and chalky to smooth and shiny. Many eggs are coloured or speckled, either for camouflage or so that the mother can tell her own eggs from impostors, which other birds may have sneaked into her nest.

## INSIDE AN EGG

A freshly laid egg consists of little but egg white and yolk. At first the chick is a tiny pink speck on the yolk, called a germ spot or embryo. Drawing on the food in the yolk and the water in the egg white, the embryo grows and a recognizable chick begins to take shape.

*The shell is semi-permeable, meaning that air and moisture can pass through it.*

*The yolk sac provides food for the embryo. It shrinks as the embryo matures.*

*The chorion encloses the growing chick and all the structures supporting it.*

*The waste sac collects the embryo's urine.*

*The embryo floats in a sac of fluid called the amnion.*

*Albumen (egg white) is a jelly-like fluid that cushions the embryo and provides a store of water.*

*The air bubble grows as the chick matures.*

*The embryo also needs warmth to grow.*

ELEPHANT
BIRD EGG

*Ground-nesting birds like kiwis lay larger eggs than birds that nest in trees. As a result, their chicks develop to a more advanced state and can run about soon after hatching.*

## A DIFFICULT LAY

Although the largest birds lay the largest eggs, small birds lay big eggs in proportion to their body size. An ostrich's egg is a hundredth of its weight, but a hummingbird's is more than a tenth of its weight. Kiwis lay proportionately the biggest eggs, at a quarter of the adult bird's weight.

CASSOWARY
EGG

STORK
EGG

EGYPTIAN
VULTURE EGG

CUCKOO
EGG

BOUBOU
SHRIKE EGG

## HOT SEAT

Birds appear to be doing little while sitting on their eggs, but they are expending up to 25% of their energy just keeping the eggs warm. Incubating eggs is especially important for birds in cold places, such as snowy owls. Their bellies have a special patch of almost bare skin which they press against the eggs to keep them warm.

*This inhospitable-looking cliff face is a good spot for a nest as it is out of the reach of many predators*

## BELLY BLANKET

Male emperor penguins balance an egg on their feet and tuck a paunchy flap of belly over the top to keep it from contact with the icy ground or air. They can go for months without eating while the mothers are away looking for food.

## EGGS THAT ROLL BACK

Guillemots lay their single eggs on rocky cliffs without nests to hold them. The eggs are cone-shaped so that they roll in a circle when bumped, which stops them falling off the cliff and smashing. Other shorebirds, such as plovers, lay groups of pointed eggs. The pointed ends fit neatly together in the middle so the plover can sit on them all at once.

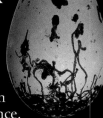

*When mallee fowl chicks hatch, they climb out of the mound and scamper away, without ever meeting their parents. Chicks can fly within hours of hatching.*

## HOME SMELLY HOME

The mallee fowl of Australia builds an incubator. It lays its eggs in a huge mound of rotting vegetation that generates heat just as a garden compost heap does. Parents adjust the temperature of the mound by adding or removing material, but have no contact with their eggs or chicks.

*Mallee fowls' mounds can reach more than 10 m (33 ft) across and are built by the males, who spend up to 11 months of the year guarding and maintaining them.*

## HATCHING OUT

Breaking out of an egg is such hard work that it takes hours or even days. To make the first crack, the chick pushes its "egg tooth" – a hard spike on its beak that it loses after hatching – against the shell with all its might.

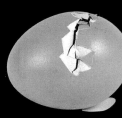

*The chick extends the crack around the egg to make a trap door.*

*The blunt end of the shell is shoved off and the chick falls out.*

*Damp feathers soon dry and fluff up. Young chickens can walk within minutes of hatching.*

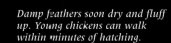

CHICK

39

# FAMILY LIFE

I N SOME WAYS, THE FAMILY LIVES OF BIRDS are much like our own. More than 90 per cent of bird species are "monogamous", which means that males and females form stable couples that work together to raise a family. In some species, such as swans, couples may stay together for life. But despite the appearance of stability and harmony, family life among birds is full of hardship, deceit, and even cruelty. Birds almost always lay more eggs than will reach adulthood, and from the moment they hatch, chicks face a struggle to survive that only the strongest can win.

## DIVORCE RATE

Family life in birds can be as complicated as in humans. Swans might appear to be a model of the perfect family, but DNA tests reveal that parents often cheat on their partners and lay eggs "out of wedlock". And if a couple has problems breeding, they may get "divorced" so each can try mating with a different partner.

## GROWING UP

Young birds fall into two main types. Ground-nesting birds such as ducks and geese have "precocial" young, which are downy and can walk and feed themselves within hours of hatching. In contrast, tree-nesting birds have "altricial" young, which are tiny, naked, and helpless. Their parents face the exhausting challenge of feeding the young until they can leave the nest.

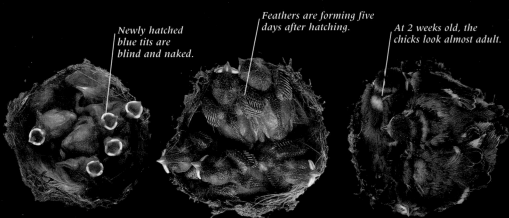

*Newly hatched blue tits are blind and naked.*

*Feathers are forming five days after hatching.*

*At 2 weeks old, the chicks look almost adult.*

## STAY-AT-HOME DAD

In jacanas, traditional sex roles are reversed. These three chicks will be cared for entirely by their father, while their mother (who may have up to three "husbands") battles with other females for control of her territory. If a jacana family wanders into the wrong area, the resident female will kill the chicks and lay new eggs for the father to rear.

## IMPRINTING
Newly hatched ducklings follow their mother, whose voice and appearance become permanently "imprinted" in their brains. If the mother isn't present, ducklings imprint on whatever else they can follow.

## PROGRAMMED TO KILL
Young birds learn some survival skills from their parents, but most knowledge is instinctive. A cuckoo never meets its parents, yet it knows how to kill the other chicks in the nest within hours of hatching.

## SIBLING RIVALRY

Birds of prey often have more chicks than can survive. The parents give most of the food to the strongest chick and turn a blind eye when it begins to bully the others. Often the well-fed chick ends up killing and eating its brothers and sisters, but sometimes the parents eat the weakest or most sickly chicks themselves.

## INSATIABLE APPETITE

Birds that feed their young work non-stop to meet their chicks' needs. A wren may make 1,000 feeding trips in a single day, and a swift may fly 1,000 km (600 miles) daily to gather enough food. Black terns spend three or four weeks flying to and from their nests, which are hidden on rafts of floating vegetation in lakes.

*A black tern returns to its chicks with a fish.*

# GAME BIRDS

THE GAME BIRDS ARE SO NAMED because they are sometimes hunted for sport. Most are good runners with strong legs, plump bodies, and powerful flight muscles. They are reluctant fliers, but in times of danger they can leap from the ground with an explosive burst of flapping. Of all the birds, game birds are the most useful to people. They are easy to catch and keep, their large muscles provide plenty of meat, and they lay eggs by the dozen.

**COURTING COCK**
The male sage grouse performs an unforgettable courtship display. With his tail spread into an amazing fan of spikes, he inflates his neck to form an enormous white ruff that swallows his head. At the same time, he lets out a deep bubbling noise. At the climax of the display, he suddenly expels all the air from his neck with a deafening whipcrack sound.

**BLUE BEAUTY**
The cobalt blue of the vulturine guinea fowl is one of nature's most brilliant hues. This species lives in flocks in dry parts of Africa and feeds on seeds and insects pecked off the ground. A fast runner, it can escape from lions on foot, but it will resort to flying if it has to. It can survive completely without water as it gets all the moisture it needs from food.

*Capercaillie cocks have a distinctive red patch just above the eyes.*

## EATING NEEDLES

Game birds swallow stones and a lot of grit to help their gizzards mash up their tough food. Grouse can digest the toughest, stringiest types of plant material. The capercaillie – the world's largest grouse – is one of the very few birds that can eat pine needles. In fact, it can get through winter on pine needles alone.

## JUNGLE FOWL

The red jungle fowl of Southeast Asia's rainforests is the wild ancestor of today's farmyard chickens and was first domesticated about 5,000 years ago. Jungle fowl, like many wild birds, occasionally lay infertile eggs, but breeders have exaggerated this habit so that domestic hens now lay hundreds of eggs a year, all of them infertile.

*A cockfight in Bali, Indonesia.*

## CHANGING WITH THE SEASONS

The willow ptarmigan changes colour with the seasons to stay camouflaged. In winter it is pure white for concealment in snow. In spring it becomes patchy, and in summer it is brown all over. In autumn it becomes patchy again as its winter plumage returns.

SPRING  SUMMER

AUTUMN  WINTER

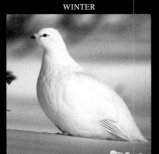

## FIGHTING FEET

Jungle fowl are polygynous, which means that one male mates with many females. Males are consequently very competitive and sometimes come to blows. When they fight, they slash at each other with sharp spurs on the feet. Wild cocks seldom injure each other, but in the sport of cockfighting they are penned together and forced to fight to the death.

## FAMILY OUTING

Quails, like most game birds, nest on the ground, laying clutches of about a dozen eggs. As they develop, the chicks communicate with each other from inside their shells to co-ordinate their growth. This way they can all hatch and leave the nest at the same time.

*The Gambel's quail of southwestern USA has a decorative plume on its head.*

## GOBBLE GOBBLE

Male turkey impress their partners by making a gobbling sound and displaying their wattles – pouches of bare skin around the head. These swell up and flush with colour as a sign of health and status.

# SONGBIRDS

ABOUT 60 PER CENT of the world's bird species belong to a group called the passerines, or perching birds. These small, compact birds typically live in trees or bushes and are distinguished by their unique feet, which enable them to perch securely on twigs and branches. Most perching birds are also known as songbirds. They use an organ called a syrinx to produce highly complex songs, usually to declare their ownership of a territory or to attract a mate. Most commonly it is the male that sings, but in some species males and females sing duets.

## DAWN CHORUS

Dawn is the noisiest time for songbirds, especially in the forests of Europe and North America during spring. Robins and redstarts usually start the singing, with finches and sparrows joining last. But why sing at dawn? One reason might be that the cool, still air helps sound to travel, making the songs more effective. Another reason may be that birds wake up before it is warm enough to hunt for insects, so they concentrate on singing instead.

## TAKING A BATH

Songbirds love to bathe, even in the middle of winter. They wash with a careful sequence of actions. First they wade into the water and dunk their heads. Then they crouch and flutter their wings to splash water across their feathers. After the bath they fly to a safe perch and preen the feathers with their beak.

*The song of the great reed warbler consists of up to 40 different phrases.*

## STEREO SOUND

A bird's voicebox, or "syrinx", creates noise as air passes over a membrane, causing it to vibrate. It is located deep down in the bird's throat, where the windpipe splits into two tubes going into the lungs. This arrangement gives birds two chambers for making sound, which means they can sing two distinct notes at the same time.

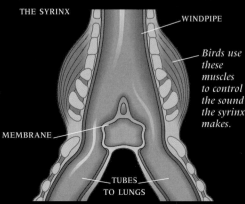

THE SYRINX

WINDPIPE

Birds use these muscles to control the sound the syrinx makes.

MEMBRANE

TUBES TO LUNGS

*The bare-throated bellbird perches at the very top of the tree so that its call will travel further.*

*The European robin stays in its territory all year and sings all year round as well.*

## RAINFOREST RACKET

Birdsong is not always pleasant to the ear. The bare-throated bellbird of Brazil has such a loud, jarring call that people call it the brain-fever bird. The African tinkerbird's maddening "song" sounds like a hammer bashing metal. Compared to the melodious songs of northern songbirds, the calls of tropical songbirds are simple, loud, and repetitive to carry through the dense rainforest canopy and remain audible over the background din of insects.

## ROWDY ROBIN

The European robin is a very noisy little bird. It is the first bird to start singing in the morning, the last to stop singing in the evening, and the most likely to be caught singing in the middle of the night, especially in places where streetlights or floodlights have confused it. Males and females both sing, but the males are noisiest.

*Songbirds' long claws can wrap around anything from thin twigs to stout branches.*

*The dipper's preen gland is larger than that of any other songbird.*

## DIPPING IN

Perching feet are not just useful for gripping branches. The dipper uses them to hold on to pebbles and so walk into fast-flowing streams where it immerses itself completely to look for aquatic insects. Its dives last about three seconds each, and it stays dry by smearing itself with water-repellent preen oil.

## PERCHING FEET

Songbirds have three forward-facing toes and one backward-facing toe, all of which are long and slender for gripping twigs of various sizes. When the legs bend, a special locking mechanism closes the claws to give a very firm grip, even when the bird is sleeping.

## HOUSE CALLS

House wrens, found in the Americas, know over 130 songs. They sing while building nests, to defend their territory, and for courting. Males can sing for 10 minutes to attract females, while those with mates sing quietly so as not to attract rival males.

## SAMPLING AND MIXING

Many songbirds improve their singing ability by stealing tunes from other species. Marsh warblers not only mimic other songs, but combine them into new compositions. They pick up hundreds of songs both from their winter feeding grounds in Africa and their European breeding territories. When the male sings, he weaves samples of many songs together to make a beautiful, fluid stream of sound.

*The European marsh warbler can mimic the songs of 99 European bird species and 113 African species.*

# KEEP AWAY!

WHEN YOU'RE UNDER ATTACK, the best form of self-defence is usually to make a quick exit. We humans rely on our legs, but birds have the advantage of flight. Once airborne, nothing can catch a bird except another bird. But there are some situations when a quick getaway is not the best solution. Eggs and chicks can't take to the wing – their parents must hide them or drive attackers away. And if a predator can follow its victim into the air, a bird may have no option but to fight.

*The frogmouth's bright pink mouth and yellow eyes can startle a predator and make it back off.*

## SAFETY IN NUMBERS

For many birds, flocking together is the first line of defence, and reduces the risk of attack for each individual bird. Predators rely on the element of surprise, but they stand little chance of getting close if there are hundreds of eyes on the lookout. In some British estuaries, red knots form flocks of more than 10,000. Birdwatchers travel hundreds of miles to see these vast flocks carpeting the mudflats and whirling around like smoke when the birds collectively take flight.

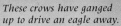

*These crows have ganged up to drive an eagle away.*

## MOBBING

Some birds gang together to "mob" predators and drive them off. They fly around the intruder, shrieking angrily and taking turns to swoop close, sometimes even making physical contact. Birds of prey, cats, and humans all regularly get mobbed.

## CAMOUFLAGE

Potoos and frogmouths stay out of sight by impersonating tree stumps. Perched bolt upright, they raise their heads, close their eyes, and let camouflaged feathers do the rest. If anything gets too close, the frogmouth opens its cavernous mouth and startles the attacker with sudden, vivid flash of colour.

A fieldfare splatters a
blackbird with a volley
of excrement.

The trumpet-
shaped entrance
tube makes the
nest completely
snake-proof.

### DEATH BY DEFECATION

Fieldfares not only mob attackers
but defecate on them – and with great
accuracy. A flock of fieldfares can cover
a predator with so much excrement that
its feathers become too soiled for flight
and it falls to the ground. There are even
reports of birds dying after fieldfare faeces
have ruined the insulating properties of
their plumage.

### SNAKEPROOF NESTS

Weaver birds
have to protect
their nests from
marauding snakes.
The openings are on
the underside, where
they are difficult to reach, and
the nests are often suspended from long
branches over water, providing a trap
for any snake that loses its grip.

### FEIGNING INJURY

Birds that nest on the ground are at great risk from
predators. The parents' only option is to make sure
predators don't find the eggs. Plovers lure foxes
away from their nests by pretending to have broken
wings and scampering away just slowly enough for
the fox to follow. Once the fox has been led astray,
the plover stages a miraculous recovery and flies off.

### HIDING IN THE REEDS

The bittern is almost impossible to see
when it wants to hide. With its head
upright, the markings on its throat blend
in perfectly with the reeds around it.
It will even sway gently in a breeze to
match the swaying reeds. The bittern's
other notable feature is the male's
extraordinary booming call, which sounds
like a foghorn and is said to be audible
from as far away as 5 km (3 miles).

### SPOT THE EGG

Plovers' eggs are superbly camouflaged, and the
type of camouflage varies enormously, even within
the same plover species. Birds that nest on sand or
gravel tend to lay speckled eggs; those that nest on
bare earth lay mottled eggs; and those that nest in
moorland lay eggs with dark spots and blotches.

# EPIC JOURNEYS

IN THE 1950s, researchers captured a Manx shearwater on an island off the coast of Wales. They took it to the city of Boston, USA, and released it. Twelve days later it was back in Wales. Many birds share this extraordinary knack of finding their way, even when it entails flying for thousands of miles across featureless ocean. It is an ability that around 10 billion individual birds put to use twice every year, when they set off on their epic migrations.

## MIGRATION AND NAVIGATION

The long journeys that birds make in autumn and spring are called migrations. Most migrating birds fly between cold and warm places, partly to avoid the winter. Their trips are exhausting and dangerous - fewer than half of first-time migrants make it back the next year. Small birds tend to fly at night, stopping during the day to rest and refuel. Birds of prey migrate by riding on thermals, so they must stay over land and travel by day.

*Migrating Canada geese in California use the Sun to tell which way is south.*

## KEY TO ROUTES

**RUBY-THROATED HUMMINGBIRD**
*Flies 3,000 km (1,900 miles) from Central America to Canada in search of food.*

**ARCTIC TERN**
*The longest route of any bird: 15,000 km (9,300 miles) from the Arctic Circle to Antarctica.*

**COMMON CRANE**
*Young common cranes learn the routes to their winter sites in Asia and Africa by flying with their parents.*

**WHITE STORK**
*By flying over Spain or the Middle East, European white storks avoid the long journey over sea, where they cannot stop to rest.*

**SNOW GOOSE**
*These birds made their way to Canada at the end of the Ice Age. Where the ice had melted, the land provided plenty of food.*

NORTH AMERICA

GULF OF MEXICO

ATLANTIC OCEAN

SOUTH AMERICA

PACIFIC OCEAN

## HOMING IN
Experiments with homing pigeons reveal that some birds have a built-in magnetic compass. This enables pigeons to find the way home from hundreds of miles away even when blindfolded. But when tiny magnets are attached to their heads to confuse them, they get lost.

## ACROSS THE GULF
The tiny ruby-throated hummingbird has to make a 20-hour, non-stop flight across the Gulf of Mexico during its treacherous trip from North to Central America. It will perish at sea if bad weather blows it off course.

ARCTIC OCEAN

EUROPE

ASIA

*Arctic terns experience more hours of daylight than any other creature because their migrations allow them to enjoy the extremely long summer days at both poles.*

AFRICA

PACIFIC OCEAN

INDIAN OCEAN

AUSTRALASIA

SOUTHERN OCEAN

### FOLLOW THE SUN
Birds that migrate by day use the Sun as a compass. They also have an internal clock, to help compensate for the Sun's movement across the sky as the day progresses. Snow geese are prompted to migrate by the Sun; when days grow longer, a hormone within the snow goose kicks in, making it restless and inclined to set off on the long journey.

*Sandhill cranes fly 6,400 km (4,000) miles from Alaska and eastern Siberia to the southern United States.*

### LANDMARKS
Some migrating birds seem to have a genetic map that tells them where to go. Cuckoos, for example, can find the way without being shown. Other birds learn the route by following a flock and memorizing landmarks, such as mountains and rivers. Landmarks based on smell and sound – such as the scent of a pine forest or the sound of crashing waves – may also help.

# OWLS

**W**ITH THEIR ROUND FACES AND HUGE EYES, owls look oddly human. They owe their baby-faced looks to their distinctive way of life. Most are creatures of the night that hunt in dusk or darkness. To find prey, they need extraordinarily good hearing and vision. The broad face works like an enormous ear and channels sound waves into ear canals hidden below the feathers. The large eyes make the most of the feeble light. Most birds have eyes on the sides of the head to see sideways, but, like humans, owls' eyes both face forwards, giving 3D vision where the fields of view overlap.

## OWL FAMILIES

In most birds, chicks hatch at the same time. Owls hatch in sequence, which gives the oldest chick an advantage. If food is in short supply, it will eat its brothers and sisters.

## BIG GULP

Like birds of prey, owls have hooked bills and sharp talons. But instead of tearing up their prey's flesh, owls swallow their victims whole. Indigestible remains such as bones and feathers are coughed up later as pellets.

*Owl pellets contain the tiny bones of their victims.*

## SELF DEFENCE

Owls usually stay well hidden during daylight hours. The long-eared owl perches motionless on a tree and looks surprisingly like a branch. If a person gets too close, it suddenly puffs itself up, spreads its wings, and glares angrily. This startling display makes the owl look bigger than it really is and gives the intruder a nasty fright.

*The bill points down so as not to obstruct vision.*

*A fringe of feathers around the face reflects high-pitched sounds.*

## SUPER SENSES

A barn owl's face is split into two discs that channel sound waves to ear canals on either side of the skull. This arrangement enables the owl to pinpoint the exact location of mice and voles deep under snow or leaves from their faint scuttling.

## HEAD TURNER

Owls can't swivel their eyes, so instead they have extra-flexible necks. They can turn their heads right round to focus their ears and locate the source of a sound.

## SILENT FLIGHT
Most owls are covered head to toe with luxurious, soft feathers. The flight feathers' velvety fringe muffles sound and allows owls to swoop silently onto prey. Dense plumage also traps warmth, saving energy so that owls get by on about 30 per cent less food than other birds of the same size.

## BURROWING OWLS
A lack of trees on North American prairies mean that burrowing owls make their homes in empty prairie dog holes. Unusually for owls, they hunt in daylight, waddling about looking for insects and worms.

# PENGUINS

IT SEEMS UNNATURAL FOR A BIRD to fly in water rather than air, but that's exactly what penguins do. Their ancestors abandoned flight more than 30 million years ago and were transformed by evolution into creatures of the sea. Wings became flippers, feet moved to the back of the body, and lightweight bones became heavy and solid to weigh them down. As well as taking to water, penguins adapted to the cold. All live in the southern hemisphere, and most live around the freezing continent of Antarctica – the coldest place on Earth.

*This iceberg has been carved into weird shapes by violent waves.*

## ICY HOMES

Some penguins need never set foot on solid ground. Chinstrap penguins often live on icebergs, and emperor penguins live on permanent ice sheets. But not all penguins live in such cold places. Galapagos penguins live on the tropical Galapagos islands on the equator, and jackass penguins live by the ocean at the edge of the Namib desert in southern Africa.

## LEAPING OUT

Getting back on land can be tricky for an animal as clumsy as a penguin, but Adelie penguins swim so fast that they fly straight out of the water up onto the ice shelf. Some penguins leap out of the water and dive back in again while swimming. This technique, which is called porpoising, seems to help them to swim faster.

*Penguins are black and white for camouflage in water. Seen from below, their bellies blend in with the bright surface; from above, their backs camouflage them against the deep water.*

## PENGUIN COLONIES

Penguins breed in large colonies called rookeries, like this king penguin rookery in South Georgia. One colony of chinstrap penguins in South Sandwich Islands is said to contain over 10 million birds. Despite the crowds, each penguin finds its mate or chick by calling and listening for a reply.

## TOBOGGANING

A penguin's feet are at the back of the body, because that's where they work best as rudders. This arrangement means they have to stand upright on land and walk with a comical waddle. On slippery ice they move more quickly by tobogganing on their bellies.

## GROUP HUG

Penguin chicks don't need sleek, waterproof coats because they don't swim, but they do need to keep warm, so they have thick downy coats that trap lots of air. Emperor penguin chicks huddle together with their backs to the wind, taking turns to stand in the middle where it's warmest.

## FLYING IN WATER

Though clumsy on land, penguins are fantastic swimmers. They shoot through the water like torpedoes, pushing with their wings and steering with their webbed feet as they twist and turn. The fastest is the gentoo penguin, which can reach 27 kph (17 mph). The champion diver is the emperor penguin, which can reach a depth of 480 m (1,570 ft) and hold its breath for 18 minutes.

# FLIGHTLESS BIRDS

FLYING IS A GREAT WAY OF FLEEING FROM DANGER and finding food, but it quickly burns through a bird's energy reserves. So, if a bird can find food and keep out of danger without having to fly, it pays to stay on the ground. Over thousands of years, many ground-dwelling birds have lost the power of flight altogether, their wings becoming withered and useless or adapted for other uses. Freed from the need to stay small and lightweight, some species evolved into the biggest birds on Earth.

### MALE MOTHER
Emus are the Australian equivalent of ostriches. As with ostriches, the males are devoted parents, incubating the eggs without getting up to eat, drink, or even defecate, and guarding the chicks for months with no help from the mother.

*The feathers are shaggy because the barbules don't zip up neatly like those of flying birds.*

*Enormous muscles power the long legs.*

### RECORD BREAKERS
Africa's ostriches don't need to fly because they can run from danger. They are the fastest birds on land and can top 72 kph (45 mph), which is twice as fast as the best Olympic sprinters. They are also the world's largest birds, with the heaviest eggs, the longest necks, the biggest eyes, and one of the longest life spans (up to 68 years). Contrary to popular belief, they never bury their heads in the sand.

*Ostriches' eyes are bigger than their brains.*

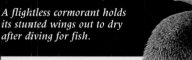
*A flightless cormorant holds its stunted wings out to dry after diving for fish.*

## ISLAND LIFE

On remote islands with no mammals, birds had few enemies and many became flightless. When explorers reached these islands, the birds proved an easy catch. The dodo of Mauritius, the Hawaiian giant goose, and New Zealand's moas were hunted to extinction. One of the few survivors is the Galapagos flightless cormorant.

## THE CURIOUS KIWI

Over time the kiwi's wings and tail have all but disappeared and its feathers have turned to fur. It lives like a badger, snuffling around forests at night and hiding in a burrow during the day. Its nostrils are at the end of a long bill, which it uses to probe the ground for worms.

*Ostriches would have to reach a ground speed of 160 kph (100 mph) to get airborne.*

*Ostriches are the only birds with just two toes, a feature that helps them sprint.*

## WINGS AS OTHER THINGS

The flightless wings of penguins, far from becoming weak with disuse, have evolved to perform a different function: instead of beating against air, they beat against water. Large wings would be slow to swim with, so they have become short, flat, and paddle-shaped. This adaptation has made penguins the fastest and most agile swimmers of any birds.

# BIRD BRAINS

PEOPLE USE THE TERM "BIRDBRAINED" to mean stupid, but birds are not as birdbrained as you might suppose. In a recent experiment at Oxford University, scientists discovered that crows have an ability that was once thought to be uniquely human: they can make tools. The crow in question figured out how to bend a piece of wire to make a hook and then use it to pull food out of a bottle. And crows are not the only birds that show uncanny signs of brain power, from feats of memory to the apparent mastery of language. But are their achievements due to true intelligence or instinct alone?

## PROBING FOR GRUBS

Woodpecker finches use cactus needles as tools to pry beetle grubs from trees. First the finch puts its ear to a branch to find out whether any tasty insects are scurrying around inside. Next, it pecks a hole in the wood to break into the beetle grub's tunnel. Finally, it pokes in the needle and tries to impale a grub and pull it out. How woodpecker finches first acquired this skill is a mystery, but experiments with caged birds have shown that other finch species can learn the same trick by copying.

*Scientists used to believe that only human beings had the capacity to make and use tools.*

*A university researcher teaches Alex to recognise a piece of wool.*

## TALKING PARROTS

Parrots are excellent mimics, but how much can they really understand? A grey parrot called Alex was trained for several years by scientists at the University of Arizona, USA. Alex can count, say "yes" and "no", and ask for things; he even seems to boss people around. Alex's trainers claim his ability shows he can think, but sceptics point out that Alex only says the names of things he can see, so he appears to have no imagination.

## HOW TO EAT BEES

Bee-eaters use a clever trick to disarm their prey. After a catching a bee, they rub it against a solid object to discharge the sting and tear off the poison sacs, which makes the bee edible. Then they toss it into their mouth in one piece. All bee-eaters know how to do this, so the technique is probably an instinct rather than a trick they have figured out by thought.

*A European bee-eater needs about 225 insects to sustain it and its young each day.*

## PLAYING DEAD

Many predators turn their nose up at carrion because the rotten meat could give them food poisoning. Some birds exploit this in an ingenious form of self-defence: they pretend to be dead. Pigeons can be made to play dead merely by tucking a head under a wing. They lie totally motionless on their backs and wait until they think the danger has passed.

## OILBIRDS

The oilbirds of South America live in pitch black caves and come out at night to feed. They use special senses rather than intelligence to cope with living in constant darkness. Like bats, they emit loud clicks that echo off solid objects and enable them to "see" by sound (echolocation).

## CHASING FIRE

Many birds are opportunists. Instead of following a rigid set of instincts, they can vary their behaviour to make the most of new feeding opportunities, including rubbish dumps and cities. In Africa, white European storks in the Masai Mara game reserve have overcome their natural fear of fire to catch small animals as they panic and flee from burning grassland.

# BIRDS AND PEOPLE

B IRDS ARE SO COMMON AND FAMILIAR that we take them for granted. The sight of a badger in a garden would provoke cries of excitement, but if a crow lands on the lawn, nobody bats an eyelid. So it might seem that birds have coped well with the changes that humans have inflicted on the world. They have adapted to life in our cities and learned to find food in gardens, farms, and rubbish dumps. But the picture is misleading. For every urban survivor, many species are struggling as their habitats disappear forever.

## WORKING BIRDS

Possibly the most ingenious way in which people use birds is to teach them to hunt for us. In Asia, falcons are trained to catch rabbits. In China, fishermen each take up to eight cormorants out on the River Li to catch fish. It takes a year to train the birds to dive down and bring back fish to the fisherman.

## GLOVE PUPPETS

The whooping crane is on the verge of extinction. In the 1800s thousands lived on the prairies of North America, but after their wetland habitats were drained, numbers plunged to just 16. Today, conservationists are trying to re-establish a viable population. The chicks are hand-reared and taught to feed by glove puppets painted to look like adults.

*These cormorants are completely tame and will dive on command.*

## FINE FEATHERS

In Papua New Guinea, the feathers of birds of paradise have been used in ceremonial headdresses for centuries. Even so, the birds are not threatened with extinction and are protected by the government.

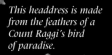

*This headdress is made from the feathers of a Count Raggi's bird of paradise.*

## REFUSE COLLECTORS

Rubbish dumps provide rich pickings for urban birds, but they are also full of dangers, from plastic bags and broken glass to nooses of tangled wire. Despite the abundance of food, only a few bird species have learned to exploit this treacherous environment. Seabirds such as herring gulls have become the dominant species on rubbish dumps.

## URBAN BIRDS

Pigeons are the most successful urban birds in the world, but what's their secret? Their ancestor is a bird called the rock dove, which nests on rocky cliffs. In the past, people built huts for rock doves to encourage them into towns and provide a source of meat. The birds lost their fear of people and soon found that buildings are just as easy to nest on as cliffs.

## ROOFTOP NESTS

In parts of Europe, white storks are considered lucky and a symbol of reliability. They are encouraged to nest on houses, and build huge stick nests on chimneys and rooftops, returning to the same nesting site every season. The myth of storks delivering babies probably arose because migrating storks arrive in Europe nine months after midsummer.

*The auk family's surviving species include puffins, razorbills, and guillemots.*

## GOODBYE GREAT AUK

The great auk was a flightless seabird that lived in the north Atlantic and looked, swam, and hunted fish in the same way as the penguins of the southern hemisphere. Being flightless, the great auk had no defences against European sailors, who hunted it to extinction. The last bird was clubbed to death by collectors in June 1844.

# STRANGE BUT TRUE

B IRDS SOMETIMES DO THE MOST PECULIAR things. Magpies and jays are famous for their strange habit of hoarding shiny trinkets such as coins and jewellery in their nests, but nobody knows why they do it. And some birds seem to do things just for fun. In Iceland, eider ducks have been seen white-water rafting down rivers and then waddling back to the start point to do it again, and Adelie penguins sometimes sledge down ice slides for a thrill. But for the most part, the way birds behave has a perfectly rational explanation, however weird and wonderful it might seem.

### ROAD RUNNER
It seems odd that a flying bird should choose to get around by running, but that's what roadrunners do, expertly. They sprint at 24 kph (15 mph) as they chase after prey, using their tails as rudders to make sharp turns without slowing down, and flipping them up in order to brake.

### KORI BUSTARD
The male Kori bustard of Africa has a few tricks for attracting mates. First he inflates his neck, then he drags his wings along the ground in a mating dance, sometimes bowing to the female. Some males will puff up all their feathers, making them look like a big, white ball. Finally, in case the females still have not noticed him, he will call with a loud booming sound across the African plains.

*The Kori bustard is one of the world's largest flying birds. The males can weigh up to 19 kg (42 lb), twice the weight of the females.*

*Hoatzin chicks have tiny claws on their elbows.*

## HANGER ON

Hoatzin chicks are strange in having claws on their wings, which they use for climbing. The claws are a throwback to the distant, evolutionary past, when the dinosaur ancestors of birds had clawed front legs.

*Hoatzins are the only tree-dwelling birds that eat almost nothing but leaves.*

## HORNBILL

Hornbills have spectacularly large bills topped by a helmet called a casque. The casque is usually hollow, but in one species it is solid ivory. Quite why such huge, cumbersome bills should evolve is a puzzle, but the bright colours suggest they may be decorations to impress potential mates.

*Blue-footed booby eggs are laid within a circle of booby droppings, which is how the birds mark out their territory – the only sign of a nest.*

## PROJECTILE VOMIT

Birds can't produce venom, but the next best thing is toxic vomit. Fulmar chicks squirt vomit at unwelcome guests like eagles or seagulls, and can hit anything within a 1.5 m (5 ft) radius. It contains acid and fish oil, which ruin seabirds' waterproofed feathers, leaving them at risk of drowning.

## BLUE-FOOTED BOOBY

This bird's ridiculous feet serve an important function. Blue-footed boobies nest on the same Pacific islands as red-footed and masked boobies, and females need to be able to tell them apart for mating. So, when a blue-footed booby is courting, he parades back and forth, stamping his blue feet to prove he belongs to the correct species.

## THE CASSOWARY'S KICK

As well as its bizarre appearance, the cassowary is also remarkable for being one of the only birds that can kill an adult human (the other is the ostrich). The dagger-like claws on its feet can disembowel a person with a single kick. The most recent fatality was in 1926, when an Australian man was kicked in the throat.

# BIRD DATA

## BIRD ORDERS

Birds make up the class *Aves*, one of the five main groups of backboned animals (vertebrates). There are around 9,700 species of birds, and closely-related species are grouped together into orders. There are 27 orders – although some experts use fewer or more orders – listed below by common name.

**Ostrich** (order Struthioniformes) 1 species

**Rheas** (order Rheiformes) 2 species

**Cassowaries and emus** (order Casuariiformes) 4 species

**Kiwis** (order Apterygiformes) 3 species

**Penguins** (order Sphenisciformes) 17 species

**Divers** (order Gaviiformes) 5 species

**Grebes** (order Podicipediformes) 22 species

**Albatrosses and petrels** (order Procellariiformes) 108 species

**Herons and relatives** (order Pelecaniformes) 65 species

**Flamingos** (order Phoenicopteriformes) 5 species

**Waterfowl** (order Anseriformes) 149 species

**Birds of prey** (order Falconiformes) 307 species

**Game birds** (order Galliformes) 281 species

**Cranes and relatives** (order Gruiformes) 204 species

**Waders, gulls, and auks** (order Charadriiformes) 343 species

**Pigeons** (order Columbiformes) 309 species

**Sandgrouse** (order Pteroclidiformes) 16 species

**Parrots** (order Psittaciformes) 353 species

**Cuckoos and turacos** (order Cuculiformes) 160 species

**Owls** (order Strigiformes) 205 species

**Nightjars and frogmouths** (order Caprimulgiformes) 118 species

**Hummingbirds and swifts** (order Apodiformes) 424 species

**Mousebirds** (order Coliiformes) 6 species

**Trogons** (order Trogoniformes) 35 species

**Kingfishers and relatives** (order Coraciiformes) 191 species

**Woodpeckers and toucans** (order Piciformes) 380 species

**Passerines** (order Passeriformes) over 5,200 species

## BIRD RECORDS

**Tallest bird** Male North African ostrich. Tallest recorded height: 2.74 m (9 ft).

**Smallest bird** Male bee hummingbird. Body length: 5.7cm (2.25 in), half of which is bill and tail.

**Largest wingspan** Wandering albatross. Largest recorded wingspan: 3.63 m (11 ft 11 in).

**Largest bill** Australian pelican. Largest recorded size: 43 cm (18.5 in).

**Heaviest flying bird** Great bustard. Heaviest recorded weight: 21 kg (46 lb).

**Most feathers** Whistling swan. Average number of feathers: 25,000.

**Fastest bird on land** Ostrich. Speed: 72 kph (45 mph).

**Fastest flying bird in a dive** Peregrine falcon. Speed: 200 kph (124 mph).

**Fastest flying bird on a level flight** Both the spine-tailed swift and red-breasted merganser have been recorded flying at 161 kph (100 mph).

**Slowest flying bird** American woodcock and Eurasian woodcock. Speed: 8 kph (5 mph) without stalling.

**Highest flight** Ruppell's griffon vulture. Highest recorded flight: 11,277 m (37,000 ft).

**Largest nest** Mallee fowl build incubation mounds of up to 4.57 m (15 ft) high and 10.6 m (35 ft) across. The amount of material in the mound would weigh about 300 tonnes.

**Smallest nest** Vervain hummingbirds' nests are the size of half a walnut shell, and bee hummingbirds have thimble-sized nests.

**Largest egg** Ostrich. Average size: 150-200 mm (6-8 in) long and 100-150 mm (4-6 in) in diameter. Average weight: 1-1.78 kg (2 lb 3 oz-3 lb).

**Smallest egg** Vervain hummingbird. Smallest recorded size: 10 mm (0.4 in) long.

**Loudest song** Male kakapo. The song can be heard 7 km (4.4 miles) away.

## GLOSSARY

**Alula** A tuft of feathers on the leading edge of a bird's wing that it raises to prevent it from stalling as it slows down.

**Barbs** Tiny side branches off a feather shaft that make up a bird's feather vane.

**Breed** To mate, lay eggs.

**Camouflage** The colour and patterning of a bird's feathers that match its particular surroundings, making it hard to see.

**Colony** A large group of birds that lives together in one place to breed or roost, or the place in which they live.

**Contour feathers** Also called body feathers, these are the small, overlapping feathers on a bird's head that give it a streamlined shape.

**Crop** A bag-like extension of a bird's gullet used to store food. It is often used to carry food back to the nest.

**Down feathers** Very soft, fine feathers that trap air close to a bird's body and help to keep it warm.

**Egg tooth** A small structure on the tip of a chick's upper bill, which it uses to crack open the eggshell when hatching. The egg tooth drops off soon after hatching.

**Extinction** The process by which living things, such as the dodo, die out completely and no longer exist.

**Flight feathers** The long feathers that make up a bird's wings and are used to fly. They can be grouped into primary feathers (on the outer wing) and secondary feathers (on the inner wing).

**Flock** A group of birds, usually of the same species, flying or feeding together.

**Gizzard** The muscular chamber in a bird's stomach, where the food that it has eaten is ground to a pulp.

**Habitat** The type of environment where a bird is normally found, such as wetland, forest, or grassland.

**Hatching** The process by which a baby bird breaks out of its egg by chipping its way through the shell with the tiny egg tooth on its beak.

**Invertebrate** A type of small animal that has no backbone, such as a worm, an insect, a spider or a crab.

**Iridescent** A glittering sheen on some feathers, and other objects, that reflects light and splits it into colours, giving the appearance of a rainbow.

**Juvenile** A young bird that is not yet old enough to breed. Its plumage often differs in colour and pattern from that of an adult.

**Migrant** A bird that travels from its feeding grounds to its breeding grounds once a year and back again.

**Migrate** To travel from one place to another in search of a plentiful food supply or good breeding grounds.

**Nectar** The sweet liquid produced by a flower that attracts birds and insects to feed from it, and so pollinate it at the same time.

**Pellet** A hard lump of indigestible bits of food, such as fur or bones, that birds such as owls cough up.

**Plumage** A bird's feathers.

**Predator** An animal that kills other animals for food.

**Preening** The way in which birds keep their feathers in good condition, drawing them through their beaks to clean and smooth them.

**Prey** An animal that is hunted and killed by another animal.

**Primary feathers** The long flight feathers on the outer half of a bird's wings that provide the power for flying.

**Scavenger** An animal, such as a vulture, that searches for dead animals to eat.

**Secondary feathers** The inner wing feathers that provide lift during flight.

**Species** A group of similar animals that can breed together and produce fertile offspring.

**Talons** The sharp, curved claws of a raptor, used for seizing prey.

**Territory** An area occupied by an animal. Birds may defend their territories against other birds of the same species.

**Tertiary feathers** A bird's innermost flight feathers, which shape the wing into the body to ensure a smooth flight.

**Thermal** A rising column of warm air, often at the edge of a cliff or hillside, on which soaring birds glide to take themselves higher into the sky.

**Wetlands** Swamps, marshes, and other wet areas of land.

## BIRD WEBSITES

**http://www.rspb.org.uk**
The website of the Royal Society for the Protection of Birds, Europe's largest wildlife conservation charity.

**http://www.birdlife.net**
The BirdLife Partnership looks at the welfare and conservation of birds across the world. The website includes news reports and project updates.

**http://www.math.sunysb.edu/~tony/birds/**
Hear birds' songs through your computer speakers by clicking on the birds. Use the map to link through to more birds across the world.

**http://birds.cornell.edu**
From the Cornell Lab of Ornithology, this site looks at bird research and provides a useful "all about birds" educational section.

**http://www.earthlife.net/birds/intro.html**
An introduction to many bird-related topics, such as migration and anatomy, with easy explanations and fun facts.

**http://www.birdsofbritain.co.uk/**
Birdwatching site for the UK including a bird guide, quizzes, and gallery.

**Please note:** Every effort has been made to ensure that these websites are suitable, and that their addresses are up-to-date at the time of going to print. Website content is constantly updated, as are website addresses – therefore, it is highly recommended that a responsible adult should visit and check each website before allowing access to a child.

## CRITICALLY ENDANGERED BIRDS

The *2002 IUCN (International Union for the Conservation of Nature and Natural Resources) Red List of Threatened Species* names 146 birds as critically endangered in the wild. The three biggest causes are habitat loss (HL), harvesting (hunted by humans; HV), and invasive alien species (AS). These are just a few of the birds on the Red List.

**Beck's petrel** Papua New Guinea; forest and sea; AS
**Blue-fronted lorikeet** Indonesia; forest; HL
**California condor** Mexico, USA; forest, savanna, shrubland; HV
**Forest little owl** India; forest; HL
**Fuertes's parrot** Colombia; forest; HL
**Giant ibis** Cambodia; forest, arable land, wetland; HL, HV
**Grey wood-pigeon** Indonesia, Malaysia; forest; HL
**Hawaiian crow** USA (Hawaiian islands); forest, shrubland; HL
**Himalayan quail** India; shrubland, grassland; HL
**Kakapo** New Zealand; forest; AS
**Little blue macaw** Brazil; forest; HL, AS, HV
**Mangrove finch** Ecuador; forest; AS
**Noguchi's woodpecker** Japan; forest; HL
**Orange-bellied parakeet** Australia; forest, coast, wetland; HL, AS
**Rudd's lark** South Africa; grassland; HL
**Siberian crane** western Asia; wetland; HL
**Slender-billed vulture** eastern Asia; forest; pollution

# Index

# Acknowledgements

Dorling Kindersley would like to thank the following people for their help with this book: Andrew O'Brien and Wildlife Art Ltd for original artworks; Chris Bernstein for compiling the index; Sarah Mills and Karl Stange for DK Picture Library research.

Dorling Kindersley would also like to thank the following for their kind permission to reproduce their photographs:

Key:
t=top, b=bottom, r=right, l=left, c=centre

**Inside book credits**

**Agency abbreviations key:**
**Alamy**: Alamy Images, **Ardea**: Ardea London Ltd, **BC Ltd**: Bruce Coleman Ltd, **DK**: DK Images, **FLPA**: FLPA-Images of Nature, **Getty**: Getty Images, **NPL**: Nature Picture Library Ltd, **OSF**: Oxford Scientific Films, **Zefa**: Zefa Picture Library

1 Zefa: H. Spichtinger. 2-3 Masterfile UK: Daryl Benson. 4-5 Ardea: Brian Bevan; 5 Science Photo Library: Jim Amos l; Alamy: Andrey Zvoznikov tl; Eric Dragesco trb; Ingrid van den Berg tr; J A Bailey trbb;

John Daniels br; Roberto Bunge tc; FLPA: Frans Lanting/Minden Pictures tcb; N.H.P.A.: Jean-Louis Le Moigne bl. 6 Alamy: Dennis Kunkel/Phototake Inc cr; 6-7 Ardea: Brian Bevan. 7 Ardea: Francois Gohier br; M. Watson ca; P. Green bl; N.H.P.A.: Steve Dalton t. 8-9 Zefa: Krahmer. 8 Ardea: Jan Baks t; Ardea: E. Mickleburgh cl. 9 Alamy: Christopher Gomersall c; Ardea: John Daniels br; R. T. Smith tl; N.H.P.A.: Alan Williams ca; Manfred Danegger caa. 10-11 Masterfile UK: Scott Tysick. 10 N.H.P.A.: Eric Soder tl; Kevin Schafer tr, Stephen Calton bl; NPL: Jeff Foot t. 11 Ardea: J.S. Dunning bl; 11 OSF: Robert Tyrrell t. 12 Ardea: J. Cancalosi tl. 12-13 NPL: Klaus Nigge. 12 Getty: Benelux Press bl. 13 Alamy: Steve Allen bra; Corbis: D. Robert rc; Kennan Ward br; 13 NPL: Pete Oxford bc. 14-15 Ardea: Peter Steyn. 14 Ardea: J. Swedberg bl; John Daniels c. 15 OSF: Eric Woods c. 15 Powerstock: t. 16-17 OSF: 16 FLPA: David Hoskings tl; N.H.P.A.: Nigel J. Dennis tr. 17 Corbis: Joe Macdonald c. 17 FLPA: R Tidman tr; Mark Newman br; NPL: Angelo Gandolfi cb; David Tipling c. 18 Ardea: John Daniels br; FLPA: BR Young br jr; Peter Davey cl. 18 OSF: Ian Wyllie/SAL cr; Scott Camazine tr. 19 Alamy: Steve Bloom

Photos; FLPA: Minden Pictures bl. 20 FLPA: Minden Pictures; 20 N.H.P.A.: Andy Rouse bl. 21 FLPA: Minden Pictures cr; Neil Bowman tr; Silvestris cl; N.H.P.A.: Bill Coster bl, bcl, bcr; OSF: Miriam Austerman br. 22-23 Alamy: Sami Sarkis. 22 NPL: Barrie Britton tl; Corbis: Keven Schafer c; OSF: William Gray bl; 23 Corbis: D. Robert & Lorri Franz tlb; Joe Macdonald trb; Peter Johnson tr; FLPA: David Hoskings tl; NPL: Pete Oxford br. 24-25 Masterfile UK: Greg Stott. 24 NPL: Thomas D. Mangelsen t. 25 Alamy: John Pickles tl; NPL: Tom Vezo cr; Tony Heald tr; OSF: Richard & Julia Kemp/SAL br; Getty: John Biustina c. 26-27 NPL: Dave Watts. 26 Corbis: Steve Kaufman tl; Bernard Castelein tl; Ardea: M. Watson br; N.H.P.A.: Roger Tidman cr. 27 NPL: Jane & Jens Eriksen br. N.H.P.A.: G I Bernard br; Laurie Campbell tr. 28-29 Alamy: Steve Bloom Images tl. 28 OSF: Gerald S Cubitt br; Corbis: Kevin Fleming c; FLPA: Frans Lanting/Minden Pictures bl. 29 Ardea: Jean-Michel Labat br; 29 BC Ltd: Gunter Ziesler tr; OSF: John Giustina bl. 30-31 Alamy: Gail Shumway; 30 Ardea: John Cancalosi cr; Mike Wilkes bl. 31 FLPA: Gerard Laci br; NPL: Jim Clare tr. 32-33 Zefa: T. Allofs. 32 Zefa: Rauschenbach bl; Alamy: Mike Lane br; Ardea: J.B & S Bottomley tl; NPL: Ashok Jain cra; Neil Lucas tl; N.H.P.A.: J. A R Hamblin c. 33 Ardea: J. Cancalosi cr; Kenneth W. Fink br; N.H.P.A.: Dave Watts tr. 34-35 NPL: Tom Vezo,

Staffan Widstrand tr. 34 Ardea: D. Parer & E.Parer-Cook bl; Bruce Coleman Inc: Norman Tomalin c. 35 BC Ltd: Tero Niemi c. 36-37 Heather Angel/Natural Visions. 36 Ardea: bl; DK: Natural History Museum tl. 37 Ardea: Chris Harvey cr; Jean-Paul Ferrero tl; NPL: Andrew Cooper c; John Cancalosi cl; Pete Oxford br; William Osborn tr. 38 DK: Harry Taylor/Natural History Museum bc, bcl; Natural History Museum br, bcll, bcr; FLPA: Frans Lanting/Minden Pictures bl; Tui De Roy/Minden Pictures bra. 39 Alamy: Steve Bloom Images cl; Ardea: B.L. Sage tr; Hans & Judy Beste br; Hans Beste cr; Corbis: Steve Kaufman cl; DK: Harry Taylor/Natural History Museum cra; Jerry Young br. 40 Auscape: bla; FLPA: David Hoskings br; P.Perry t; Zefa: H. Reinhard tl. 41 FLPA: A R Hamblin c. Getty: Benelux Press l; 42 NPL: Jeff Foott l; Zefa: Winfried Wisniewski. 43 Ardea: Chris Knights tr; BC Ltd: Jane Burton tr; Corbis: W. Perry Conway crb. 43 FLPA: L Lee Rue cr; S. McCutcheon cr; Winfried Wisniewski cb; NPL: Colin Seddon cl; Jeff Foott cl; John Downer bl; John De Meester cl; OSF: Roland Mayr. 45 Alamy: Mike Lane cc; Ardea: Chris Knights bl; Masterfile UK: Tim Fitzharris br; NPL: Nick Gordon tl. N.H.P.A.: Stephen Dalton tr; OSF: Colin Milkins cl. 46-47 N.H.P.A.: Eric Soder. 47 Ardea: Chris Knights c; FLPA: Foto Natura Stock cr; William S. Clark bl. 47 Ardea: Christer Fredriksson cr; FLPA: Richard Brooks cr; NPL: Brian Lightfoot; David

Kjaer cl; N.H.P.A.: Manfred Danegger tl. 48-49 Getty: John Warden. 48 FLPA: S&D&K Maslowski br. 49 FLPA: D Kinzler br; OSF: Peter Hawkey/SAL tr; Zefa: W. Wisniewski bl. 50 FLPA: Minden Pictures t; NPL: Dietmar Nill cr; Ingo Arnott t; Tom Vezo bl; N.H.P.A.: Rich Kirchner br. 51 BC Ltd: Kim Taylor. Corbis: W. Perry Conway cl. 52-53 Alamy: David Tipling/ Image State t. 52-53 FLPA: Minden Pictures b. 52 BC Ltd: Tom Schandy l; N.H.P.A.: B & C alexander t. 53 Ardea: Graham Robertson cr; FLPA: Terry Andrewartha t; Zefa: Wisniewski l. 54-55 NPL: Tony Heald. 54 Heather Angel/Natural Visions. tr. 55 FLPA: Tui De Roy/Minden Pictures tr; N.H.P.A.: Daniel Cox br; Robin Bush cr. 56-57 OSF: Tui De Roy. 56 The Alex Foundation: Joe McDonald c; NPL: John Downer tl; OSF: Alain Christof cr; Juan M Renjifo/AA cl. 58-59 Corbis: Jonathan Blair. 58 Ardea: Don Hadden bl; Jack A. Bailey br; NPL: Martin Harvey tl; OSF: Hans Reinhard/OKAPIA cr. 59 Ardea: Bob Gibbons bl; NPL: Bristol City Museum br. 60 Ardea: John Cancelossi l; National Geographic Image Collection: Beverly Joubert. 61 Ardea: Kenneth W. Fink trb; FLPA: F De Noover/Foto Natura Stock tr; Masterfile UK: Greg Stott bc; NPL: John Downer cl; OSF: Alan Root/SAL br; Getty: Andy Caulfield tr. 62-63 Getty: Joseph Van Os.

All other images © Dorling Kindersley.
For further information see:
www.dkimages.com